THE WINDI

Eternity

Where does the road wend?
Further than you can see.
Where does the stream end?
In the far-distant sea.
Whither does time extend?
Into eternity

EVELYN CAPEL

For Irmeli, Albion, Kristian, Sebastian,
Rupert, Francesca and Oscar

THE WINDING ROAD

Family treasury of poems and verses

Compiled by Matthew Barton

Hawthorn Press

The Winding Road © 2004 Matthew Barton

Matthew Barton is hereby identified as the author of this work in accordance with Section 77 of the Copyright, Designs and Patent Act, 1988. He asserts and gives notice of his moral right under this Act.

Published by Hawthorn Press, Hawthorn House, 1 Lansdown Lane, Stroud, Gloucestershire, GL5 1BJ, UK
Tel: (01453) 757040 Fax: (01453) 751138
info@hawthornpress.com
www.hawthornpress.com

Cover illustration by Helen Williams
Cover design by Hawthorn Press
Design and typesetting by Lynda Smith at Hawthorn Press, Stroud, Glos.
Printed in the UK by The Cromwell Press, Trowbridge, Wiltshire

Printed on acid-free paper from managed forests

Every effort has been made to trace the ownership of all copyrighted material. If any omission has been made, please bring this to the publisher's attention so that proper acknowledgment may be given in future editions.

British Library Cataloguing in Publication Data applied for

ISBN 1 903458 47 1

CONTENTS

FOREWORD

My earliest memory of language is of rhymes and verses, first spoken by my mother and father, then by me, as I learned them off by heart, read them and made up my own. It seemed to set the rhythm of life. That's what poetry does: touches on experiences and expresses each one in a way which makes them personal, unique and transcendant. It is a form of worship, yet can be agnostic; it can record feelings, yet also invoke and share those feelings. It is something the human being craves from the earliest moment of communication, and yet, tragically, it can be lost so soon, and the emptiness remains as a sense of some unidentified lack.

This carefully and tenderly selected collection of verses and poems not only takes the family through the main rites of passage, but through many of the spaces in between too. It reflects expectation, hope, the child's excitement of discovery, the mother's bonding with her infant, the adolescent breaking away into adulthood. Most joyfully, it is full of love and wonder for our world.

What pleasure awaits those who not only dip into this book at random, but who also search for the particular poem or verse which has personal meaning. What a gift for the family – and how wonderful to think of a new book growing with the family and being passed on, thoroughly finger-smudged, tear-stained and page-turned.

As Thomas Traherne says in his poem 'Wonder',

> A native health and innocence
> Within my bones did grow,
> And while my God did all his glories show,
> I felt a vigour in my sense
> That was all spirit.

JAMILA GAVIN

INTRODUCTION

These poems and verses accompany the journey from conception through to late adolescence. Marking many stages on that winding road, they offer insight and courage to parents, carers, teachers and children for the shared voyage of love and discovery, or simply record special moments of awakening and awareness. While many of the poems are not directly intended for younger children themselves, the inspiration they give may flow directly, if subtly, into parenting.

The sections on birthdays, morning verses, graces and evening verses, however, contain poems for young children themselves to speak with parents. From a very young age children respond to rhythmic patterns of speech that can, when lovingly spoken first to and then with them, wrap them in a secure sense of oneness with the world.

Simple phrases often contain truths that we easily overlook. The coinage 'mother tongue' reminds us that we drink in language unconsciously and effortlessly from those closest to us, even before birth, and certainly in the first years of life. My mother first gave me a feeling for the mysterious power of language when I was young. If I try to remember far enough back – which I can't consciously – I get a sense of warmth surrounding me in a full tone of voice, a shawl of language inseparable from the caring that accompanied it. Later she shared her own love of language with me, in stories, nursery rhymes, poems and songs, giving me a lifetime gift, a deep source to draw from.

Then I remember learning certain poems by heart (interesting that we do not say 'by head'). Although my family subscribed to no religion, I had to learn psalms at school. I still remember the compelling strength and beauty in some of those words from the King James Bible. Another poem I learned was T.S. Eliot's 'Journey of the Magi'. Though I might have been eleven or so by then, I still recall the excitement of the shape, texture and atmosphere of the words, even if their intellectual meaning was neither so apparent nor important to me. Whether or not connected with that poem, the idea of a transforming 'journey' – though not tied to a particular religion – has been one that has accompanied me since, and finds its echo in the title of this book. It also seems an apt metaphor for every reading of a poem, in which the destination of conscious understanding is no more important than travelling the road itself, with its immediacy of experience, every bump and rut.

I am sure that children cope much better than we usually believe with words they don't immediately understand. My 6-month-old grandson already responds to and, I think, recognises Yeats's *The Lake Isle of Inisfree* or Frost's *Stopping By Woods on a Snowy Evening*. Poetry, if it is worth the name, is a deep, intuitive experience of sound, rhythm and layers of meaning which we cannot fully analyse in adult concepts. I do not believe that a young child will suffer harm from hearing any of the poems in this book. On the contrary, even if they are beyond his or her immediate grasp, they can open ear and heart to the beauty, power and music of language.

In the later sections of the book, for older children and their parents, many of the poems address the experience of adolescence, the emerging sense of separation and self that develops at this age, and finally both the loss and release in the sound of the spreading of wings.

The journey this book takes with parents and children will, I hope, make it into a magical piece of luggage into which one can dip and draw out just the right gift at the right time: whether for confirmation, courage, insight or celebration.

An anthology such as this is inevitably defined as much by what it leaves out as what it includes. I regret that for cost or space reasons some poems are only represented as excerpts, but I trust that readers will be moved here and there to seek out the full, original versions.

This is very much a mixed bag, drawn from many different sources. Verses by that prolific poet Anon jostle cheerfully with meditations and poems by older or modern poets. What they all share, though, is a love of the child's journey and a sense that adults are blessed and privileged to accompany it.

MATTHEW BARTON

PART I

THE CLAY THAT SHAPES:
BEFORE BIRTH

These poems and prayers all relate in some way to the mysteries that occur before birth: mysteries of love and origin, of creation springing from a deep, unseen source. Who knows what is really at work as a child comes towards birth? Yet we can accompany this journey in our thoughts and feelings, so that the unborn child senses our mood of wonder and welcome.

Yes

Last night I dreamed again of Adam returning
To the garden's scented, bubbling cauldron.

Eve was beside him,
Their shadows were cut adrift
And the hum of bees was in their blood.

And the world was slow and good and all
The warm and yawning newness of their flesh
Was fixed for ever in the glow of "Yes".

BRIAN PATTEN

I am the Song

I am the song that sings the bird.
I am the leaf that grows the land.
I am the tide that moves the moon.
I am the stream that halts the sand.
I am the cloud that drives the storm.
I am the earth that lights the sun.
I am the fire that strikes the stone.
I am the clay that shapes the hand.
I am the word that speaks the man.

CHARLES CAUSLEY

Self-conceiving

The mist is clearing as I enter it.
I'm starting to see what I need,
need what I see:
I come to the crown of a moment, gaze
on my new life's promised land:
mother to ground and enfold me, father to send
the spear of me beyond myself.
Father and mother: my need is starting to bind
you to each other. As yet you do not see
I'm here and urging the deeper motions in you.
You've forgotten you know me, but I'm in
the undercoil of your hearing, in the blind
spring of your seeing, the pit of your gut,
your muscles' dreaming flight.
I'm tying you into me, drawing up
your deeper will from unknown depths
to serve me, give me shape between you, make
love into life.

MATTHEW BARTON

Good Wish

Power of raven be thine,
Power of eagle be thine,
    Power of the Fiann.

Power of storm be thine,
Power of moon be thine,
    Power of sun.

Power of sea be thine,
Power of land be thine,
    Power of heaven.

ANON
TRANSLATED FROM THE GAELIC
BY ALEXANDER CARMICHAEL

For mothers-to-be

Spirit stars working from the heights,
sun power creating in unfolding breadths,
God strength striving out of the depths:
bless, heal, enliven
the human seed and build
the temple of the body.

Out of spirit light's free sway,
in soul strength poured out by love,
through faith-wrought will for sacrifice,
let me endow the human child, divine
offspring, with body's nourishment,
soul's growth, the future of the earth.

RUDOLF STEINER

A mother's prayer

Into my will
let there pour strength,
into my feeling
let there flow warmth,
into my thinking
let there shine light,
that I may nurture this child
with heart's deep spring of love.

ANON

I watched the jump you made

I watched the jump you made from far away star
you balanced on the pivot of my mind
you were tipped
landing like the warmth of light on cold waters.
I lie round the warmth of you
you lie like a rounded pebble
causing my rising
like bread
brooding
on the weight of air
you turn my world to silence
I've found your porcelain hand
resting in mine
and I won't let go.

FRANCESCA KALLIOMÄKI-BARTON
AGED 17

Ultrasound

You develop before our eyes:
palm raised in greeting, rising
into focus out of underoceans.
Pharaoh with mysterious scroll, translucent
traveller from interior space: you summon
past and future into the fine
presence of a face. You're surfacing,
taking soundings, slowly engaging with gravity: a short
journey away from us, already we feel the pull
of love you're hauling us towards you with.

MATTHEW BARTON

Prayer

Our baby's heart, on the sixteen-week scan
was a fluttering bird, held in cupped hands.

I thought of St. Kevin, hands opened in prayer
and a bird of the hedgerow nesting there,

and how he'd borne it, until the young had flown
– and I prayed: this new heart must outlive my own.

KATHLEEN JAMIE

Pregnant Pause

Drawn outside to smell the waking earth
I feel you wake
to flit against me, bird
or fish or babe, this spring
you are all three,
and I who sought fulfilment in my words,
wishing for a moment to be God,
and give new form a voice,
find now the poetry I strove for
in the blossom and the tulips' fire
in your fledgling life within me.

DOROTHY BAIRD

Sea Change

A chambered nautilus hangs in an inland sea.
Ariel: trapped by rough magic of the heart,
Tuned now to the humming music of the gut.
A muffled dead-march drumbeat summons him
To put on flesh, give up eternity.

Growing Caliban-gross, the huge head
Of our delicate monster hears itself ears,
Sees eyes and they bud; feels fingers, they flower.
Under this ancient fish, this blind, dumb worm,
Hides the lost one; the sea-girl; the wonder;
Waiting to return.

Till, moon-pulled, tempest-wracked, a mariner
Borne on the amniotic flood,
She beaches on the roaring, undreamt shore:
Cries like a seagull as the midwife cuts the anchor –
O brave new world. O pain. O blood.

CATHERINE PETERS

From Prayer before Birth

I am not yet born: O hear me.
Let not the bloodsucking bat or the rat or the stoat or the
    club-footed ghoul come near me.

I am not yet born, console me.
I fear that the human race may with tall walls wall me,
    with strong drugs dope me, with wise lies lure me,
        on black racks rack me, in blood-baths roll me.

I am not yet born; provide me
With water to dandle me, grass to grow for me, trees to talk
    to me, sky to sing to me, birds and a white light
        in the back of my mind to guide me…

LOUIS MACNEICE

Dialogue with the Unborn

We talked yesterday,
You and I,
I told you that
For my birthday
Your father gave me
An African violet,

A dark potent flower
With the pollen
In yellow bags;

And I told you
How a butterfly
Came through the door
Unexpectedly,
One of the last
Coming in from the cold.

I told you
I was twenty-seven:
I thought you had
A right to know.

Then I listened,
And it came:
The speech in your feet
Sudden and strong.

GABRIEL MILLAR

Before Birth

May the soul of the child
be given to me,
as you will it,
out of spirit worlds.

After Birth

And may the soul of the child
be guided by me,
as you will it,
into spirit worlds.

RUDOLF STEINER

A SHOCK OF LIGHT: BIRTH

Birth: not only the beginning of new life for our child, but a new life for us too, an enormous change in our lives. A time of vivid, painful joy, when the world itself and everything around us seems reborn, clear and fresh, as though an original force returns to bless us.

The Birthnight

Dearest, it was a night
That in its darkness rocked Orion's stars;
A sighing wind ran faintly white
Along the willows, and the cedar boughs
Laid their wide hands in stealthy peace across
The starry silence of their antique moss:
No sound save rushing air
Cold, yet all sweet with Spring,
And in thy mother's arms, couched weeping there,
     Thou, lovely thing.

WALTER DE LA MARE

From Red Letter Day

…I watched a surgeon
thrust white hands deep into your mother's stomach,
scrabble about as if there were finishing touches
to be made – a bow to be tied, a feature kneaded
into shape – or as if he were simply gathering up,
this late summer, two handfuls of autumn leaves.
From the gallery I held that feeling
of the leaves holding together between my palms
(a few falling from the edges, but nothing
could break my concentration now) as I raised them
carefully up and up, the blood-smell of autumn
ripening in the air, till with a shout
they were over my head and released
into the wind. Pure joy! A dove
from red silken rags; a head, so
perfect, so beautiful. So it's true, love
can read the writing on the furthest star:
my eyes focusing with the intensity of heart,
body and soul. Then the body in the middle
of this white, this green aquarium light, the body
a warm, a russet, a maple glow. Oh,
I saw you for both of us, saw the beautiful boy
rising from his mother's innards, she spread,
spread and used like earth, as like a rose tree,
he seemed to rise by himself through the air,
his pulsing stem the cord rooted
in his mother's earth.

TOM POW

From The Million Sufferings of the Light

I remember my daughter opening her eyes for the first time. An astonishment. A great shock of light. Never before seen. Never again. As we all are – windows into. Unique articulations of the light.

PAUL MATTHEWS

For a mother to speak for her child

Into you may light stream that can grasp you.
I attend its rays with my love's warmth,
I think with my best, most joyful thoughts
of your heart's stirrings.
May they strengthen you,
sustain you,
clarify you.

I want to gather up the steps
you'll take in life into my joyful thoughts
so that they link with your will for life,
so that this will can strengthen, find itself
everywhere in the world,
ever more through itself.

RUDOLF STEINER

From Frost at Midnight

Dear Babe, that sleepest cradled by my side,
Whose gentle breathings, heard in this deep calm
Fill up the interspersèd vacancies
And momentary pauses of the thought!
My babe so beautiful! it thrills my heart
With tender gladness, thus to look at thee,
And think that thou shalt learn far other lore,
And in far other scenes! For I was reared
In the great city, pent 'mid cloisters dim,
And saw nought lovely but the sky and stars.
But *thou* my babe! shalt wander like a breeze
By lakes and sandy shores, beneath the crags
Of ancient mountains, and beneath the clouds,
Which image in their bulk both lakes and shores
And mountain crags: so shalt thou see and hear
The lovely shapes and sounds intelligible
Of that eternal language, which thy God
Utters, who from eternity doth teach
Himself in all, and all things in himself.
Great universal teacher! He shall mould
Thy spirit, and by giving make it ask.
        Therefore all seasons shall be sweet to thee,
Whether the summer clothe the general earth
With greenness, or the redbreast sit and sing
Betwixt the tufts of snow on the bare branch
Of mossy apple tree, while the night thatch
Smokes in the sun-thaw; whether the eave-drops fall
Heard only in the trances of the blast,
Or if the secret ministry of frost
Shall hang them up in silent icicles
Quietly shining to the quiet moon.

SAMUEL TAYLOR COLERIDGE

Infant Joy

'I have no name:
I am but two days old.'
What shall I call thee?
'I happy am,
Joy is my name.'
Sweet joy befall thee!

Pretty Joy!
Sweet joy, but two days old!
Sweet Joy I call thee.
Thou dost smile,
I sing the while,
Sweet joy befall thee!

WILLIAM BLAKE

Infant Sorrow

My mother groan'd! my father wept.
Into the dangerous world I leapt:
Helpless, naked, piping loud:
Like a fiend hid in a cloud.

Struggling in my father's hands,
Striving against my swaddling bands,
Bound and weary I thought best
To sulk upon my mother's breast.

WILLIAM BLAKE

'The Angel that presided o'er my birth'

The angel that presided o'er my birth
Said, 'Little creature, form'd of Joy and Mirth,
Go love without the help of any Thing on Earth.'

WILLIAM BLAKE

Let-Down
For Medbh McGuckian

When my milk came in, oh not *my* milk, the child's –
well whose? can I say clearly? though I did
taste it once, a thin hazelnut water –
well, when it came in, it stood blue-veined in my breasts
and I could not express it. My breasts were as hard to grip
as Hallowe'en apples, the ones you hang on strings
from a clothes airer hauled to the ceiling, and try to bite.
Oh my breasts were hard as Bramleys
and my nipples tender as a cut.
The child could not catch on. How would she, the scrap?
And she wept, and the other babies round me wept
for the milk I had to spare, but could not express.

When I no longer could lay my arms by my sides
and the midwife was threatening a drug to suppress lactation
it came to me, the dark shed in Rathmullen
and the child I was that summer, pressing all
the left side and ear of her head against
the leathern flank of the cow, pulling, learning
the rhythm, the teat music
as the milk jet jangled onto galvanised metal
or drove richly into the foam of itself.
That double note. The sound of relief.
The nee-naw rhythm of rescue.

The child that was me couldn't, of course, get the hang.
But the mother I suddenly am hears the pitch of percussion
deepen as the bucket fills, its long diminuendo…
My shirt front's wringing, and when I unfasten my bra
Two jets of milk rise in two crossing arcs
Right over the head of my nuzzling wavery child.

CATHERINE BYRON

Nursery Blues

I do not know where it is,
the warm smell I reach for
in the night, the warm milk
that keeps the screams away from me.

She's gone. The door took her away.
I hate doors, they are mouths
eating my mother, the yawn
of moondark swallowing the sky.

The others play with their toes,
find their thumbs to warm them,
burble in their baskets.
But there's a wail in me,

a giant sound that keeps on coming
and my thumb is too small
to stop its flood, and the shoulder
my cheek lies on and the hand

that smoothes my back
do not smell of her,
and even the light,
without her, is black.

DOROTHY BAIRD

When Chloe Was Small And We So Tired

In April we heard the ice begin to break.
   The ice broke.
      Mud: the road dissolved. Then June.
         Blackflies as we tilled the ground.

As we tilled the ground the world warmed,
   the lake warmed.
      Crayfish marched around in their exoskeletons.
      Otters fished from our dock at dusk.

At night, aurora borealis,
   vague and milky to the north.
      At five a.m., Chloe
      awake and echoing.

     *   *   *

The earliest hour of light:
   forest sloping green to shore,
      the lake metal gray,
         a silver mist giving water

a goodbye kiss; water at rest.
   Chloe asleep
      on her sleeping father's chest.
      Toward the smallest cove,

I guided my canoe. A slight wind.
   Lilies, reeds. Herons posing,
      herons flying over
         the main body of water.

The mildest current
      bringing me to cove's edge.
            Canoe gliding over clouds,
                  over galaxies of frog and minnow eggs.

           *   *   *

Thinking I've studied this
      small world enough,
            I steer my canoe homeward,
                  toward the larger lake.

But each time I reach
      the mouth of the cove,
            I'm turned back,
                  slight wind like a flat hand

sending the canoe around again.
      I work to gather
            speed, momentum, will;
                  look for surface rifts,

for a current that might
      explain my helplessness;
            consider panicking:
                  one more lost paddler,

lacking sense or experience,
      who might be forced
            to portage overland for miles,
                  milk for her baby swelling,

falling from her breasts—
      then, something
            almost asked for
                  gets me out of there:

I do nothing different
      but the boundary's breached.

CARRIE GRABO

Lullaby

Sleep, my babe, and do not cry:
The brook runs hidden by twilight,
And the hawthorn bark will not feel
The teeth of the sheep until morning;
The bindweed closes on the darkening fence.

Sleep my little house martin,
Tucked in your nest;
The bat is awake, veering between stars;
A fox lopes through the field –
The downwind scent of the hen
Puts greed in his feet.
Reeking of cud the cow spirals to sleep
On the cowmown grass.

Sleep my babe, and do not cry;
You cannot see from your cradle how
The moon shrinks as it rises
To the top of the sky.

GABRIEL MILLAR

RAINING DOUBLE BLESSINGS DOWN: BLESSING, NAMING AND BAPTISM

'To name is to acknowledge. It is to identify, single out, distinguish, separate and endow with meaning. It is also to empower and bless…In the act of naming we can try to connect with the true being of a child.'

CAROLINE SHERWOOD

From Birth Baptism

A wavelet for thy form,
A wavelet for thy voice,
A wavelet for thy sweet speech;

A wavelet for thy luck,
A wavelet for thy good,
A wavelet for thy health;

A wavelet for thy throat,
A wavelet for thy pluck,
A wavelet for thy graciousness;
Nine waves for thy graciousness.

ANON
TRANSLATED FROM THE GAELIC
BY ALEXANDER CARMICHAEL

Gaelic Blessing

Deep peace of the running waves to you,
Deep peace of the flowing air to you,
Deep peace of the quiet earth to you,
Deep peace of the shining stars to you
Deep peace of the shades of night to you,
Moon and stars always giving light to you,
Deep peace of Christ, the son of peace, to you.

ANON

Christening Verse

The light of your thinking
begins to shine
upon the path of your life.
I will guide it gently
into your spirit's stream.

The warmth of your feeling
begins to flow
over the ground of your life.
I will guide it gently
into your soul's weft.

The strength of your will
begins to work
in the limbs of your life.
I will guide it gently
into your whole being.

RUDOLF STEINER

For my daughter, Anouk Finn, on the day of her naming

The name Anouk means grace
and in its sound
a note of mystery is found, like a
call upon the wind.

And grace you have in abundance, little one…
grace of the fresh-tilled earth
and the dappled, dancing sun.

The name Finn means fair…
…of face, of colour, of deed – in you
I see all three.
Yet as I sound the name I taste
the salt of the sea.

These are but inklings of a mother,
dancing shapes behind my eyes.
However you grow to meet your name
I look forward to surprise.

CLAUDINE WHITING

Christening

We mark this day our wonder
that you have come, teaching us
to be your father and your mother,
opening our eyes to your enormous joy.

We remember your birth
when you burst upon us from the crumpled womb
and breathed, calm and still,
as though this was no more than you'd expected,
while we held you as though you'd break.

We name you Thomas, but doubt not
that we love you, nor that your heart,
like the hills, has its own wisdom.

We name you Arthur: be the king
and leader if you will, but be too the farm boy
who smiles when the sun rises.

We name you William, and ask no more
of you, than the flowers, sweet William,
for they become themselves
                        and gladden our hearts.

Thomas Arthur William: our son,
our sun: may we two shine
like the moon, in your light.

DOROTHY BAIRD

Birthdays

For my daughters: Celeste and Amber Sherer ,
born on September 5, 1989

They are me.
They are of me and they are more than me.
They are two sweet sips of beauty
steeped in the language of dreams,
earth, sky, fog, clouds and undiluted blue streams of girl song.
Their innocence sings of worlds I once knew.
They are my first and second born in one birth.
The first an airy indigo guru full of wisdom and sight.
The second a solid ginger prayer bundle
burning with an intense fire.
They are two but more than two.
They are my many poetic stories happening at once.
I was once a simple woman with not much voice, a hollow bell.
Motherhood struck the chord brought me forward with sound,
inducted me into the tribe of poetic prayer tongue,
transformed me into a holy roller of words and worlds,
straddled me across the abyss of both pain and joy,
marinated me in the juice of what my daughters have made me;
a fierce mother Eagle, a Hawk, but mostly a Phoenix rising
wingspan wide with the one true color, compassion.
A poet mama bird feeding herself, her babies and others on words.
So, when I speak of multiple birth, I am including myself too.
My girlself grew from the food of womantalk
and wise from woman ways,
growing upward and round
with the power of circles, embracing hearts, arms and hips
with the carriage of large loads:
babies, joy, and the dark root of sorrow.

On this journey of becoming momma, mom and mother
I have gone beyond bone,
the passage brought me back with a stretched soul;
made me wide by my only two true epic poems,
I am kept alive by their telling
and my wings are flared with hope and redemption.
They show me how in everything we do
no matter what, we touch the world.
I am a rough rock smoothed by kissing water
raining double blessings down
with the best of both earth and sky.

GLENIS REDMOND

Prayer for a Young Child

Spring put a sprig in his mind,
Prosper his enterprises.
May the hand that gropes in the roosting box
Lift out an egg.

His hope blow like a rose in the morning,
And may the grunt of thunder
And the rush of rain
Relieve the pressure of the summer sun.

May his foot find a way
Among the fallen leaves,
As the sun blazes over the Severn
And the night falls cold.

The nip of winter hone his sword
And exercise his centre;
The stars of the dark flare in his eye,
The frost preserve his resolutions.

Unleasher of seasons,
Keep in the nooks a wink
For the murky-hearted,
A rush-light for the lonely.

Light him at last
To sleep in his scallop,
The sea singing renewal
And the life to come.

GABRIEL MILLAR

Wishes for Anouk

May the earth always cradle your feet, and your purpose.
May your joy careen in streams.
May the air carry your songs…
        …and your silence;
May the firelight rock your dreams.

May you wear your earthly beauty with grace,
        knowing there are gifts above.
May you walk alone and know peacefulness,
May you walk with another and know love.

May you find a pebble that fits just right in your palm,
May it warm with your passionate fire.
May your air carry laughter…
        …and songs to the birds,
May your earth cradle another.

May your heart know the incandescence of God surrounding you,
May your childhood weave wings for your soul.
May the wishes of a mother be borne lightly,
        as your story unfolds.

CLAUDINE WHITING

Peace

Peace between neighbours,
Peace between kindred,
Peace between lovers,
In love of the King of life.

Peace between person and person,
Peace between wife and husband,
Peace between woman and children,
The peace of Christ above all peace.

Bless, O Christ, my face,
Let my face bless every thing;
Bless, O Christ, mine eye,
Let mine eye bless all it sees.

ANON
TRANSLATED FROM THE GAELIC BY
ALEXANDER CARMICHAEL

PART II

TO SHINE ON EARTH:
A YOUNG CHILD'S BIRTHDAY

What does a birthday mean to a very young child? Even an infant can feel, without quite understanding, that this is a celebration of his or her unique individuality that is gradually working its way into life, gradually taking increasing hold on the world around, and grasping it in every sense.

Monday's child is fair of face,
Tuesday's child is full of grace,
Wednesday's child will reap and sow
Thursday's child has far to go,
Friday's child is loving and giving
Saturday's child works hard for its living,
But the child who is born on the Sabbath day
Is lucky and bonny and good and gay.

ANON

For the night before a birthday

When I have said my evening prayer,
And my clothes are folded on the chair,
And mummy* switches off the light,
I'll still be …years old tonight.
But from the very break of day,
Before the children rise and play,
Before the darkness turns to gold
Tomorrow I'll be … years old.
… kisses when I wake,
… candles on my cake.

ANON

A goodnight kiss for the five-year-old
To send her to sleep and to dreaming.
And blessings on the six-year-old
Who'll climb out of bed in the morning.

ANON

*Or, of course, Daddy!

Birthday morning

Softly, softly waken
To your special day.
Let the bright sun lead you,
Lead you on your way.

Softly, softly waken
To your day of birth.
Take my hand and come with me
To greet the shining earth.

The stones, beasts, birds surround you,
The fresh grass underfoot
Your future steps await you:
The world is sweet and bright.

ANON

Lighting birthday candles

From the stars
I did come down
bearing my light
to light a crown
of shimmering stars
to shine on earth;
today's the day I came to birth.

ANON

They chose me
For adopted children

I have two mothers,
My birth mother and my Mum.
I have two fathers,
My blood father and my Dad.

But of all the babies born
In the big wide world,
My Mum and Dad chose ME.

I have two days,
My Birthday and my Chosen Day.
I get two cakes
And have my friends to tea.

But of all the babies born
In the big wide world,
My Mum and Dad chose ME.

I am the one
The child they went to find.
I am the one
To make their family,

For of all the babies born
In the whole wide world
My Mum and Dad chose ME.

JAMILA GAVIN

For the night following a birthday

Soon I will sleep
and dream towards
the humming stars;
and of all nights
this night is when
I'll find myself
deep-rooted where
the stars grow wings,
enfold me with
the life that grows
in me and sings.

ANON

ARISE, ARISE!
MORNING VERSES WITH
YOUNG CHILDREN

Morning is like childhood itself – the fresh spring of life. These verses welcome each new day, and at the same time the dawning energy and life which young children feel in themselves.

Pawnee Prayer

Earth our mother, breathe forth life
All night sleeping
Now awakening
In the east
Now see the dawn.
Earth our mother, breathe and waken
Leaves are stirring
All things moving
New day coming
Life renewing.

ANON

The great sun is rising
Above the green hill,
His golden light shining
Over meadow and rill.

He shines on the flowers,
They wake one by one
And spread out their petals
To greet the great sun.

ANON

The Robin's Song

God bless the field and bless the furrow,
Stream and branch and rabbit burrow,
Hill and stone and flower and tree,
From Bristol Town to Wetherby –
Bless the sun and bless the sleet,
Bless the lane and bless the street,
Bless the night and bless the day,
From Somerset and all the way
To the meadows of Cathay;
Bless the minnow, bless the whale,
Bless the rainbow and the hail,
Bless the nest and bless the leaf,
Bless the righteous and the thief,
Bless the wing and bless the fin,
Bless the air I travel in,
Bless the mill and bless the mouse,
Bless the miller's bricken house,
Bless the earth and bless the sea,
God bless you and God bless me!

ANON

Pippa's Song

The year's at the spring;
The day's at the morn;
Morning's at seven;
The hill-side's dew-pearled;
The lark's on the wing;
The snail's on the thorn;
God's in His heaven –
All's right with the world!

ROBERT BROWNING

Hark! Hark! The lark at heaven's gate sings,
And Phoebus 'gins arise,
His steeds to water at those springs
On chaliced flowers that lies;
And winking Mary-buds begin
To ope their golden eyes;
With everything that pretty is,
My lady sweet arise!*
Arise, arise!

WILLIAM SHAKESPEARE

*For a boy, you could substitute: My sweet lad arise!

Over the earth is a mantle of green
Over the green the dew
Over the dew are the arching trees
Over the trees the blue.
Across the blue the scudding clouds
Over the clouds the sun
Over it all is the love of God
Blessing us every one.

ANON

Birds in the air,
Stones on the land,
Fishes in the water,
I'm in God's hand.

After ANGELUS SILESIUS

The golden sun so great and bright
Warms the world with all its might.
It makes the dark earth green and fair,
Attends each thing with ceaseless care.
It shines on blossom, stone and tree,
On bird and beast, on you and me.
O may each deed throughout the day,
May everything we do and say
Be bright and strong and true,
O golden sun, like you!

ANON

Spring Prayer

For flowers that bloom about our feet;
For tender grass, so fresh and sweet
For song of bird and hum of bee;
For all things fair we hear or see
Father in heaven, we thank thee!

For blue of stream and blue of sky;
For pleasant shade of branches high;
For fragrant air and cooling breeze;
For beauty of the blossoming trees,
Father in heaven we thank thee!

RALPH WALDO EMERSON

Seeing the sun
I think God's spirit,
moving my hand
God's soul lives in me,
taking a step
God's will walks in me.
In all people whom I see
God's soul lives;
and lives also
in creature, plant and stone.
Fear can never touch me
when I think God's spirit,
when I feel God's soul,
when I walk in God's will.

RUDOLF STEINER

The sun's bright light
illumines day
after dark night:
the soul's strength now
awakens from
sleep's quiet rest:
you, my soul,
give thanks to the light,
within it shines
the power of God;
you, my soul, arise,
do spirited deeds.

RUDOLF STEINER

The through-cloud shiner:
may he
shine through
light through
glow through
warm through
me too.

RUDOLF STEINER

Fruit in a blossom
And petals in a seed,
Reeds in a river bed
Music in a reed:
Stars in a firmament,
Shining in the night,
Sun in a galaxy,
And planet in its light;
Bones in the rosy blood
Like land in the sea.
Marrow in a skeleton,
And I in me.

OWEN BARFIELD

Sun

The eye of the great God,
The eye of the God of glory,
The eye of the King of hosts,
The eye of the King of the living
Pouring upon us
At each time and season,
Pouring upon us
Gently and generously.

Glory to thee,
Thou glorious sun.

Glory to thee, thou sun
Face of the God of life

ANON
TRANSLATED FROM THE GAELIC BY
ALEXANDER CARMICHAEL

Song of the Dawn

Now comes the hour foretold, a God
      gift-bringing, a wonder-sight.
Is it a star new-born and splendid
      up-springing out of the night?
Is it a wave from beauty's fountain
      up-flinging foam of delight?
Is it a glorious immortal bird that is
      winging hither its flight?
Is it a wave, high-crested, melodious,
      triumphant, breaking in light?
Is it a bloom, rose-hearted and joyous,
      a splendour risen from night?
Is it a flame from the world of the gods,
      and love runs before it,
      a quenchless delight?

Let the waves break,
Let the star rise,
Let the flame leap,

      Ours, if our hearts are wise,
      to take and keep.

ANON
FROM THE IRISH

53

Home

When in the lovely hullabaloo of morning,
the cock o' the house has no doubt
as to his bugle duty,
and the hens bwrrk bwrrk
at the hustling sun,
the cats drool in the long grass as
the martins bellyflop from their nests.
Coffee and perfume and buttered toast
honey through the house,
sticking in curtains and corners –
incense of the kitchen and incarnation.
The children tumble up
and squabble down,
and the door of the day thuds open
like a shop.

GABRIEL MILLAR

BREAD IS A LOVELY THING TO EAT: GRACES

The way we do even the simplest, most ordinary, everyday things – such as sitting down to a meal together – can help children connect with the world as a good, generous and sustaining place, and give them a sense of wholeness and belonging. I remember garbling though a grace at my primary school –

'Forwhatweareabouttoreceivemaythelordmakeustrulythankfulamen'

– which certainly didn't give me anything except a sense of something imposed on me by adults who had little reverence themselves. If, as parents, we can engender in ourselves real thankfulness towards the earth – often rare nowadays – our children feel this and are nourished by it.

A few of the verses that follow are not suitable as graces, but were included because they relate to the theme in some way.

I saw a stranger today.
I put food in the eating-place
And drink in the drinking-place
And music in the listening place.

In the holy name of the Trinity
He blessed myself and my family.

And the lark said in her warble:
Often, often, often
Goes Christ in the stranger's guise.
O, oft and oft and oft,
Goes Christ in the stranger's guise

FROM THE GAELIC

A Child's Grace

Thank you for the earth so sweet,
Thank you for the things we eat,
Thank you for the birds that sing,
Thank you, God, for everything.

ANON

Some hae meat and canna eat,
And some wad eat that want it;
But we hae meat and we can eat,
And sae the Lord be thanit.

ROBERT BURNS

American Indian Prayer

Great spirit, Creator of all that we
see, hear, smell, taste, and all that we touch;
Mother Earth, Makē Ina, womb of all beings
provider of all our needs.

Keeper of the West, home of the thunder people,
place where Grandfather Sun sleeps at night.

Keeper of the North, home of the great white giant,
from where fresh breezes blow.

Keeper of the East, land of the rising sun,
home to the big red mountain.

Keeper of the South, land that we always face,
from where the growing warmth comes.

I pray to the stone peoples, the green peoples, the winged peoples,

I pray to the four-legged peoples, the swimming peoples,
the crawling peoples, and to the star peoples.
I pray to all who give us food, clothing, medicine, dwellings, and designs.

To the ancestors of all the peoples,
I pray for their help in keeping us in balance, and
teaching us the ways of the Creator and Mother Earth.

To the star peoples, Grandfather Sun, Grandmother Moon
I give thanks that they light our way in times of darkness.

To all these peoples I give thanks for all the gifts and help
I get in my life each and every day.

ANON

Before the flour the mill
Before the mill the grain,
The sun, the earth, the rain
The beauty of God's will

ANON

Substance of earth,
Essence of light,
Grace of heaven:
In us unite.

FRANCIS EDMUNDS

For the deep earth that cradles the seed
For the rain that brings forth the green leaves
For the stars that give form to the flowers
For the warm sun that ripens the fruit:
For all this goodness and beauty
Our heavenly father we thank thee

GLADYS HAHN

In the deep, dark earth, plants stir,
green shoots sprout in the vital air,
fruits ripen through the sun's bright power;

so stirs the soul in the shrine of the heart,
so sprouts the spirit's strength in the light of the world,
so ripens our human strength in the brightness of God.

RUDOLF STEINER

Sunlight streams through
far breadths of space,
birdsong rings out
through open fields of air,
the gift and grace of plants
sprout from the being of earth;
and, in gratitude, human souls
lift themselves to the spirits of the world.

RUDOLF STEINER

On each grain is written
The name of the eater
The giver is the one
The giver is God.

HINDI GRACE

The Harvest

The silver rain, the shining sun,
The fields where scarlet poppies run,
And all the ripples of the wheat
Are in the bread that I do eat.

So when I sit for every meal
And say a grace, I always feel
That I am eating rain and sun
And fields where scarlet poppies run.

ALICE C. HENDERSON

It's not the bread that feeds us –
What feeds us in the bread
Is God's eternal word
Is spirit and is life.

ANGELUS SILESIUS

Blessings on the blossom,
Blessings on the root,
Blessings on the leaf and stem
Blessings on the fruit.

ANON

Lovely Things

Bread is a lovely thing to eat –
God bless the barley and the wheat!

A lovely thing to breathe is air –
God bless the sunshine everywhere!

The earth's a lovely place to know –
God bless the folks that come and go!

Alive's a lovely thing to be –
Giver of life, we say – bless thee!

H .M. SARSON

From The Traveller

Blest be that spot, where cheerful guests retire
To pause from toil, and trim their evening fire;
Blest that abode, where want and pain repair,
And every stranger finds a ready chair;
Blest be those feasts with simple plenty crowned,
Where all the ruddy family around
Laugh at the jests or pranks that never fail,
Or sigh with pity at some mournful tale;
Or press the bashful stranger to his food,
And learn the luxury of doing good.

OLIVER GOLDSMITH

Love's Fabric

For Chris and Signe Schaefer on their departure for the city

May this tablecloth be spread
   first
      with your family bread

then a grace come about you
    that whenever you shake
       crumbs out at the door

the sparrows might carry
    sweetness to the sour
      salt to the savourless.

Thy cup runneth over
    into the unfamiliar
      by-ways of the city.

Say simply *tablecloth be spread*
    and all hearts
      can feast there.

It is love's fabric –
    many strands of us
      woven together.

PAUL MATTHEWS

Love

Love bade me welcome: yet my soul drew back,
  Guilty of dust and sin.
But quick-eyed Love, observing me grow slack
  From my first entrance in,
Drew nearer to me, sweetly questioning,
  If I lacked anything.

A guest, I answered, worthy to be here:
  Love said, You shall be he.
I, the unkind, ungrateful? Ah my dear
  I cannot look on thee.
Love took my hand, and smiling did reply
  Who made the eyes but I?

Truth Lord, but I have marred them: let my shame
  Go where it doth deserve.
And know you not, says Love, who bore the blame?
  My dear, then I will serve.
You must sit down, says Love, and taste my meat:
  So I did sit and eat.

GEORGE HERBERT

SLEEP'S UNLATCHED DOOR: EVENING AND PRAYER

Verses that mark stages in the day give children a sense of security in the recurring, breathing pattern of things. After the day's busy activities, the evening journey towards sleep can be a gentle, magic time, though also a time when fears surface that need soothing. Sleep is also a return to our deeper, unconscious selves, and young children sense this intuitively. Evening poems and prayers enclose and enfold children. They are a way of rounding off and making peace with the day, and helping a child slip off into wholesome sleep.

This Moment

A neighbourhood.
At dusk.

Things are getting ready
to happen
out of sight.

Stars and moths.
And rinds slanting around fruit.

But not yet.

One tree is black.
One window is yellow as butter.

A woman leans down to catch a child
who has run into her arms
this moment.

Stars rise.
Moths flutter.
Apples sweeten in the dark.

EAVAN BOLAND

From The Song of Hiawatha

At the door on summer evenings
Sat the little Hiawatha;
Heard the whispering of pine-trees,
Heard the lapping of the water,
Sounds of music, words of wonder;
"Minne-wawa!" said the pine-trees,
"Mudway-aushka!" said the water.
Saw the firefly, Wah-wah-taysee,
Flitting through the dusk of evening.
With the twinkle of its candle
Lighting up the brakes and bushes;
And he sang the song of children,
Sang the song Nokomis taught him:
"Wah-wah-taysee, little firefly,
Little, flitting, white-fire insect,
Little, dancing, white-fire creature,
Light me with your little candle,
Ere upon my bed I lay me,
Ere in sleep I close my eyelids!"
Saw the moon rise from the water
Rippling, rounding from the water,
Saw the flecks and shadows on it,
Whispered, "What is that, Nokomis?"
And the good Nokomis answered:
"Once a warrior, very angry,
Seized his grandmother, and threw her
Up into the sky at midnight;
Right against the moon he threw her;
Tis her body that you see there."
Saw the rainbow in the heaven,
In the eastern sky the rainbow,
Whispered, "What is that, Nokomis?"

And the good Nokomis answered:
"'Tis the heaven of flowers you see there;
all the wild-flowers of the forest,
all the lilies of the prairie,
when on earth they fade and perish,
blossom in that heaven above us."
When he heard the owls at midnight,
Hooting, laughing in the forest,
"What is that?" he cried in terror;
"What is that," he said, Nokomis?"
And the good Nokomis answered:
"That is but the owl and owlet,
Talking in their native language,
Talking, scolding at each other."

HENRY WADSWORTH LONGFELLOW

Evening

She sweeps with many-coloured brooms –
And leaves the shreds behind –
Oh, housewife in the evening west –
Come back and dust the pond!

You dropped a purple ravelling in –
You dropped an amber thread –
And now you've littered all the east –
With duds of emerald!

And still she plies her spotted brooms –
And still the aprons fly –
Till brooms fade softly into stars –
And then I come away.

EMILY DICKINSON

The Moon

The moon was but a chin of gold
A night or two ago –
And now she turns her perfect face
Upon the world below.

Her forehead is of amplest blond –
Her cheek like beryl stone –
Her eye unto the summer dew
The likest I have known.

Her lips of amber never part –
But what must be the smile
Upon her friend she could bestow
Were such her silver will!

And what a privilege to be
But the remotest star!
For certainly her ways might pass
Beside your twinkling door.

Her bonnet is the firmament –
The universe her shoe –
The stars the trinkets at her belt –
Her dimities of blue.

EMILY DICKINSON

From my head to my feet
I am the image of God,
from my heart to my hands
I feel God's breath,
speaking with my mouth
I follow God's will.
When I see God
everywhere, in mother, father,
in all loving people,
in creatures, stones,
no fear is mine,
just love for all
that is around me.

RUDOLF STEINER

Prayer at the Ringing of Evening Bells

To wonder at beauty,
safeguard truth,
revere what is noble,
resolve to do good:
this leads human beings
in life to their goal,
in deeds to what's right,
in feeling to peace,
in thinking to light;
and teaches them trust
in the workings of God,
in all that exists
in the universe,
in the innermost soul.

RUDOLF STEINER

All the stars in the sky
speak of spirit's beauty;
the sun in cosmic space
speaks of spirit's power;
the moon in night's dark cloak
speaks of spirit's paths.

RUDOLF STEINER

The stars shine –
it is night;
stillness fills space,
all is quiet.
I feel the stillness
I feel the quiet;
In my heart,
In my head,
God speaks,
Christ speaks.

RUDOLF STEINER

Matthew, Mark, Luke and John
Bless the bed that I lie on:
Four corners to my bed,
Four angels there lie spread:
Two at my head, two at my feet,
One at my heart, my soul to keep.

ANON

Now I lay me down to sleep,
I pray thee, Lord, my soul to keep;
Thy love go with me all the night
And wake me with the morning light.

ANON

Finger Verse

Here's a cottage in the wood
And here's the place where the chimney stood
Here's the smoke from the fire bright
And here are the curtains closing tight
As everyone inside says good night.

WINNIE MOSSMAN

Hindu Cradle Song

From groves of spice,
O'er fields of rice,
Across the lotus-stream,
    I bring for you,
    Aglint with dew,
A little lovely dream.

Sweet, shut your eyes,
The wild fireflies
Dance through the fairy neem,*
    From the poppy bole
    For you I stole
A little lovely dream.

ANON

*Neem means a lilac tree in Hindustani

Sweet and Low

Sweet and low, sweet and low,
    Wind of the western sea,
Low, low, breathe and blow,
    Wind of the western sea!
Over the rolling waters go,
Come from the dying moon, and blow,
    Blow him again to me;
While my little one, while my pretty one, sleeps.

Sleep and rest, sleep and rest,
    Father will come to thee soon;
Rest and rest, on mother's breast,
    Father will come to thee soon;
Father will come to his babe in the nest,
Silver sails all out of the west
    Under the silver moon:
Sleep, my little one, sleep my pretty one, sleep.

ALFRED LORD TENNYSON

Silver

Slowly, silently, now the moon
Walks the night in her silver shoon;
This way, and that, she peers and sees
Silver fruit upon silver trees;
One by one the casements catch
Her beams beneath the silvery thatch;
Couched in his kennel, like a log,
With paws of silver sleeps the dog;
From their shadowy cote the white breasts peep
Of doves in a silver-feathered sleep;
A harvest mouse goes scampering by,
With silver claws and silver eye;
And moveless fish in the water gleam,
By silver reeds in a silver stream.

WALTER DE LA MARE

Prayer of St. Patrick

God be with me
God within me
God behind me
God before me
God beside me
God around me
God to comfort me and restore me.

God beneath me
God above me
God in quiet
God in danger
God in hearts of all that love me
God in mouth of friend and stranger.

ANON
FROM THE IRISH

I see the moon
And the moon sees me:
God bless the moon,
And God bless me.

ANON

The night is so dark
But the stars shine so bright
I pray you my angel
Be with me this night

ANON

The Guardian Angel
For fear before sleep

Angel of God who has charge of me,
Dear Father of mercy, and all the saints
Enfold me safely this dark night,
Drive from me every temptation and danger,
Surround me on the tempestuous sea,
And in the narrows, crooks and straits,
Keep thou my coracle,
Keep thou it always.

Be thou a bright flame before me,
Be thou a guiding star above me,
Be thou a smooth path below me,
And be thou a kindly shepherd beside me,
Today, tonight and forever more.

CELTIC PRAYER

On a Dark Road

Her eyes the glow-worm lend thee.
The shooting stars attend thee,
    And the elves also,
    Whose little eyes glow
Like the sparks of fire, befriend thee.

No will-o'-the-wisp mislight thee,
Nor snake or slow-worm bite thee;
    But on thy way
    Not making a stay
Since ghost there's none to affright thee.

Let not the dark thee cumber
What though the moon does slumber!
    The stars of the night
    Will lend thee their light
Like tapers clear, without number.

ROBERT HERRICK

From The Starlight Night

Look at the stars! look, look up at the skies!
    O look at all the fire-folk sitting in the air!
    The bright boroughs, the circle-citadels there!
Down in dim woods the diamond delves! the elves'-eyes!
The grey lawns cold where gold, where quickgold lies!
    Wind-beat whitebeam! airy abeles set on a flare!
    Flake-doves sent floating forth at a farmyard scare!
Ah well! It is all a purchase, all is a prize.

GERARD MANLEY HOPKINS

Fairies' Song to Titania

You spotted snakes with double tongue
Thorny hedgehogs, be not seen;
Newts and blind-worms, do no wrong,
Come not near our fairy queen.

Philomel, with melody
Sing in our sweet lullaby.
Lulla, lulla, lullaby, lulla, lulla, lullaby:
Never harm,
Nor spell nor charm:
Come our lovely lady nigh;
So, good night, with lullaby.

Weaving spiders, come not here;
Hence, you long-legg'd spinners, hence!
Beetles black, approach not near;
Worm nor snail, do no offence.

WILLIAM SHAKESPEARE

Psalm 23

The Lord is my shepherd; I shall not want.
He maketh me to lie down in green pastures:
he leadeth me beside the still waters.
He restoreth my soul:
he leadeth me in the paths of righteousness for his name's sake.
Yea, though I walk through the valley of the shadow of death,
I will fear no evil: for thou art with me;
thy rod and thy staff they comfort me.
Thou preparest a table before me in the presence of mine enemies:
thou anointest my head with oil; my cup runneth over.
Surely goodness and mercy shall follow me all the days of my life:
and I will dwell in the house of the Lord for ever.

From Night

The sun descending in the west,
The evening star does shine;
The birds are silent in their nest,
And I must seek for mine.
> The moon like a flower
> In heaven's high bower,
> With silent delight
> Sits and smiles on the night.

Farewell green fields and happy groves,
Where flocks have took delight.
Where lambs have nibbled, silent moves
The feet of angels bright;
> Unseen they pour blessing,
> And joy without ceasing
> On each bud and blossom
> And each sleeping bosom.

WILLIAM BLAKE

Bed in Summer

In winter I get up at night
And dress by yellow candlelight.
In summer, quite the other way,
I have to go to bed by day.

I have to go to bed and see
The birds still hopping on the tree,
Or hear the grown-up people's feet
Still going past me in the street.

And does it not seem hard to you,
When all the sky is clear and blue,
And I should so much like to play,
To have to go to bed by day?

ROBERT LOUIS STEVENSON

Good Night

No more work and no more play,
Every toy is put away,
Ended is the lovely day,
Then – good night!

Drink the milk all white and creamy,
Have your bath all warm and steamy
Close your eyes all tired and dreamy,
Then – good night!

Through the window stars are peeping,
From their holes the mice are creeping,
Your white bed is soft for sleeping,
Then – good night!

RUTH AINSWORTH

The House of Dream

Candle, candle, burning clear,
Now the House of Dream draws near;
See what shadowy flowers move
The solitary porch above;
Hark, how still it is within,
Though so many guests go in.

No faint voice will answer make
While thy tapering flame's awake.
Candle, candle, burning low,
It is time for me to go.
Music, faint and distant, wells
From those far-off dales and dells.

Now in shoes of silence I
Stand by the walls of witchery;
Out then, earthly flame, for see,
Sleep's unlatched her door to me.

WALTER DE LA MARE

On the Tree-Top

Slowly it leaves, flowers – the silent
uprush of blossom, the flowing
apple-sap of sleep
so lovely in a child –
I follow the breath
growing full, whole, deep;
the gentle, stranded driftwood
limbs cast lightly up.

MATTHEW BARTON

PART III

FEET FIND A WAY: FIRST MILESTONES

The following poems mark some of the stages in a journey through the first eight years or so of childhood. We usually talk of growing 'up', but growing 'down' makes equal sense: down into our distinct and earthly selves, taking root.

From The Prelude

Was it for this
That one, the fairest of all rivers, loved
To blend his murmurs with my nurse's song,
And, from his alder shades and rocky falls,
And from his fords and shallows sent a voice
That flowed along my dreams? For this, did'st thou,
O Derwent! travelling over the green plains
Near my sweet birthplace, did'st thou, beauteous stream
Make ceaseless music through the night and day
Which with its steady cadence, tempering
Our human waywardness, composed my thoughts
To more than infant softness, giving me
Among the fretful dwellings of mankind
A knowledge, a dim earnest of the calm
That Nature breathes among the hills and groves…

WILLIAM WORDSWORTH

From Wonder

How like an angel came I down!
How bright are all things here!
When first among his works I did appear
O how their glory did me crown!
The world resembled his eternity,
In which my soul did walk;
And everything that I did see
Did with me talk.

The skies in their magnificence,
The lively, lovely air;
Oh how divine, how soft, how sweet, how fair!
The stars did entertain my sense,
And all the works of God, so bright and pure,
So rich and great did seem,
As if they ever must endure
In my esteem.

A native health and innocence
Within my bones did grow,
And while my God did all his glories show,
I felt a vigour in my sense
That was all spirit. I within did flow
With seas of life like wine;
I nothing in the world did know
But 'twas divine. […]

The streets were pav'd with golden stones,
The boys and girls were mine,
Oh how did all their lovely faces shine!
The sons of men were holy ones,
In joy and beauty they appeared to me,
And every thing which here I found,
While like an angel I did see,
Adorn'd the ground.

Rich diamond and pearl and gold
In ev'ry place was seen;
Rare splendours, yellow, blue, red, white and green,
Mine eyes did everywhere behold.
Great wonders cloth'd with glory did appear,
Amazement was my bliss,
That and my wealth was everywhere:
No joy to this!

THOMAS TRAHERNE

From The Third Century

All appeared new, and strange at first, inexpressibly rare and delightful and beautiful. I was a little stranger, which at my entrance into the world was saluted and surrounded with innumerable joys [...]

The corn was orient and immortal wheat, which never should be reaped, nor was ever sown. I thought it had stood from everlasting to everlasting. The dust and stones of the street were as precious as gold: the gates were at first the end of the world. The green trees when I saw them first through one of the gates transported and ravished me, their sweetness and unusual beauty made my heart to leap, and almost mad with ecstasy, they were such strange and wonderful things: The Men! O what venerable and reverend creatures did the aged seem! Immortal Cherubims! And young men glittering and sparkling Angels, and maids strange seraphic pieces of life and beauty! Boys and girls tumbling in the street, and playing, were moving jewels. I knew not that they were born or should die; But all things abided eternally as they were in their proper places. Eternity was manifest in the Light of the Day, and something infinite behind everything appeared which talked with my expectation and moved my desire. The city seemed to stand in Eden, or to be built in Heaven. The streets were mine, the temple was mine, the people were mine, their clothes and gold and silver were mine, as much as their sparkling eyes, fair skins and ruddy faces. The skies were mine, and so were the sun and moon and stars, and all the World was mine; and I the only spectator and enjoyer of it. I knew no churlish proprieties, nor bounds, nor divisions: but all proprieties and divisions were mine: all treasures and the possessors of them.

THOMAS TRAHERNE

Norfolk Shore

Up over the dyke and we're
emptied out across the windwaste, hurled
against the heaving, pebble-spittling
sea-milk surge.

You poke your new fingers
into the wet flints and shingle –
the great grey seacow
thuds thunder above you;
for once though I'm fearless, I know
you're safe, you belong
here between me and the ocean – your ears and eyes
opening like anemones.

MATTHEW BARTON

Two-Year-Old

Catherine in a blue pinafore
stands on a chair. Dishwashing's over.
She strokes a bottlebrush of clear water
around the sink and says, *Red.*

She dips the brush in the milk bottle
and strokes again and says, *Yellow.*
How carefully, how busily
she paints the sink with clear water.

I know she knows it's just her pleasure
to make two worlds of the one world.
There's nothing wrong with mottled porcelain –
but what's the matter with red and yellow?

She loads the brush, that little maestro,
and speaks with the same and such decision
I stare at the mottled porcelain –
her pinafore isn't half so blue.

NORMAN MACCAIG

Beattie Is Three

At the top of the stairs
I ask for her hand. O.K.
She gives it to me.
How her fist fits my palm,
A bunch of consolation.
We take our time
Down the steep carpetway
As I wish silently
That the stairs were endless.

ADRIAN MITCHELL

Lao Waking

Who comes in the snow-light,
Who comes in the morning?
Who sings at my side as the sun
climbs up over the hill?

A blue tit, a primrose,
a plaited polly –
gallant you come, gay-haired,
assuaging my sorrow.

As though no coercions had ever oppressed
the vulnerable heart of man –
no slaughter, no madness,
no falling from God.

If I reive your loveliness,
claiming your lustre for my own,
it is part of a progress
towards consolation:

who sees you remembers how ice melts
and every year elvers come,
finding the Severn,
from the Sargasso Sea.

GABRIEL MILLAR

From The Shepherd's Calendar

The reapers leave their beds before the sun
And gleaners follow when home toils are done
To pick the littered ear the reaper leaves
And glean in open fields among the sheaves.
The ruddy child nursed in the lap of care
In toils rude ways to do its little share,
Beside its mother poddles o'er the land
Sun burnt and stooping with a weary hand
Picking its tiny glean of corn or wheat
While crackling stubbles wounds its legs and feet.
Full glad it often is to sit awhile
Upon a smooth green baulk to ease its toil,
And feign would spend an idle hour to play
With insect strangers, to the moiling day
Creeping about each rush and grassy stem,
And often wishes it was one of them
In weariness of heart that it might lie
Hid in the grass from the days burning eye…
Whilst its expecting mother stops to tie
Her handful up and waiting his supply
Misses the resting younker from her side
And shouts of rods and more of threats beside…
Leaving his pleasant seat he sighs and rubs
His legs and shows scratched wounds from piercing stubs
To make excuse for play but she disdains
His little wounds and smiles while he complains.
And as he stoops adown in troubles sore
She sees his grief and bids him sob no more
As bye and bye on the next Sabbath day
She'll give him well earned pence as well as play
When he may buy almost without a stint
Sweet candied horehound cakes and pepper mint

Or streaking sticks of luscious lollipop
What ere he chooses from the tempting shop
Within whose diamonds window shining lie
Things of all sorts to tempt his eager eye -
Rich sugar plumbs in phials shining bright
In every hue young fancies to delight
Coaches and ladies of gilt ginger bread,
And downy plumbs and apples streaked with red:
Such promises all sorrows soon displace
And smiles are instant kindled in his face...

JOHN CLARE

There's a Girl

There's a girl
running with boots on.
Here's a me watching with eyes.

There is the grass green and seen.
Here is me seeing the grass green.

Trees – so treeful.
Me so meful.

What does it mean to be green and a tree?
What does it mean to be me to be me?

PAUL MATTHEWS

Thumb

I'm five and it's Christmas
when I decide to give up

sucking my thumb –
the same thumb I suppose

as this squat one
that holds the pen,

though thinner certainly – I can remember
the sucked look of the thing

like a stone a few tides away
from transparency. Thirty-one years on

I suck it again and find
its memory longer than mine:

gliding with ease back up
into the womb of my mouth, it plugs

the gap in the dyke through which –
O so long since –

the world came pouring in.

MATTHEW BARTON

Whitsun Ride

Around your head you'd tied the fountain
of a large white silk scarf and rode
your first bicycle down the pavement;
I was coming along behind
to catch you up if need be –
all I caught
were the undulating shadows of a wind
silvering off your headlong
rush into the morning, leaving me
empty mouthed and open handed.

MATTHEW BARTON

A Good Play

We built a ship upon the stairs
All made of the back bedroom chairs,
And filled it full of sofa pillows
To go a-sailing on the billows.

We took a saw and several nails,
And water in the nursery pails;
And Tom said, 'Let us also take
An apple and a slice of cake';
Which was enough for Tom and me
To go a-sailing on, till tea.

We sailed along for days and days,
And had the very best of plays;
But Tom fell out and hurt his knee,
So there was no one left but me.

ROBERT LOUIS STEVENSON

My Mother said that I never should
Play with the gypsies in the wood,
The wood was dark; the grass was green;
In came Sally with a tambourine.

I went to the sea – no ship to get across;
I paid ten shillings for a blind white horse;
I up on his back and was off in a crack,
Sally tell my Mother I shall never come back.

ANON

My girl's a jack-o'-lantern
My girl's a jug
She's got four teeth missing
From her pretty little mug.

GABRIEL MILLAR

Registers

Out of the warm primordial cave
of our conversations, Jack's gone.
No more chit-chat under the blankets
pegged over chairs and nipped in drawers.

Throughout his first five years an ear
always open, at worst ajar,
I catch myself still listening out
for sounds of him in the sensible house

where nothing stirs but the washing machine
which clicks and churns. I'm loosening his arms
clasped round my neck, detaching myself
from his soft protracted kiss goodbye.

Good boy, diminishing down the long
corridors into the huge unknown
assembly hall, each word strange,
even his name on Miss Cracknell's tongue.

MICHAEL LASKEY

'Yann says Marlon's got a magic pig'
'I don't believe him'
'Me neither'
'Well, I half do'
'Me too'

GABRIEL MILLAR

My Quiet Place

My quiet place is my cupboard.
I like my dresses hanging down like leaves
Hanging down in my face.
I put my face in my dresses.
It is dark and quiet and peaceful.
The leaves start tickling my nose.
I laugh and jump out of the cupboard.

FLORENCE KAYLL
AGED 6

Isn't My Name Magical?

Nobody can see my name on me.
My name is inside
and all over me, unseen
like other people also keep it.
Isn't my name magical?

My name is mine only.
it tells I am individual,
the one special person it shakes
when I'm wanted.

Even if someone else answers
for me, my message hangs in air
haunting others, till it stops
with me, the right name.
Isn't your name and my name magic?

If I'm with hundreds of people
and my name gets called,
my sound switches me on to answer
like it was my human electricity.

My name echoes across playground,
it comes, it demands my attention.
I have to find out who calls,
who wants me for what.
My name gets blurted out in class,
it is terror, at a bad time, because somebody is cross.

My name gets called in a whisper
I am happy, because
my name may have touched me
with a loving voice.
Isn't your name and my name magic?

JAMES BERRY

Selfhood Discovered

Knee-deep in a field of buttercups
Surrounded by light and gold
Far off in my childhood playtime
I witnessed my Ego unfold.

Lost to the laughter of playmates
Startled, I knew myself grown
Separate in my existence –
Different, uniquely alone.

Alone with the buttercups shining
In golden splendour around;
Alone, in that holy moment
With the sunlight streaming down.

Wisdom and truth eternal
Flashed through my tremulous heart
As I stood there in time suspended
Consciously stood apart.

Children's voices calling
Brought me to earth again,
I carried my secret knowledge
Wrapped in my seven year frame.

Long since that magical moment
But radiant the memory will stay –
How the sun and the light and the buttercups
Shone round me that hallowed day.

MARGARET GUDEMIAN

A Song of Riches

What will you give to a barefoot lass,
Morning with breath like wine?
Wade, bare feet! In my wide morass
Starry marigolds shine.

Alms, sweet Noon, for a barefoot lass,
With her laughing looks aglow!
Run, bare feet! In my fragrant grass
Golden buttercups blow.

Gift, a gift for a barefoot lass.
O twilight hour of dreams!
Rest, bare feet, by my lake of glass,
Where the mirrored sunset gleams.

Homeward the weary merchants pass,
With the gold bedimmed by care.
Little they wise that the barefoot lass
Is the only millionaire.

KATHARINE LEE BATES

From Home at Grasmere

While yet an innocent Little-one, with a heart
That doubtless wanted not its tender moods,
I breathed (for this I better recollect)
Among wild appetites and blind desires,
Motions of savage instinct my delight
And exaltation. Nothing at that time
So welcome, no temptation half so dear
As that which urged me to a daring feat.
Deep pools, tall trees, black chasms and dizzy crags,
And tottering towers, I loved to stand and read
Their looks forbidding, read and disobey,
Sometimes in act, and evermore in thought.

WILLIAM WORDSWORTH

From The Prelude

Fair seed-time had my soul, and I grew up
Foster'd alike by beauty and by fear;
Much favor'd in my birthplace, and no less
In that beloved Vale to which, ere long,
I was transplanted. Well I call to mind
('Twas at an early age, ere I had seen
Nine summers) when upon the mountain slope

The frost and breath of frosty wind had snapp'd
The last autumnal crocus, 'twas my joy
To wander half the night among the cliffs
And the smooth hollows, where the woodcocks ran
Along the open turf. In thought and wish
That time, my shoulder all with springes* hung,
I was a fell destroyer. On the heights
Scudding away from snare to snare, I plied
My anxious visitation, hurrying on,
Still hurrying, hurrying onward; moon and stars
Were shining o'er my head; I was alone
And seem'd to be a trouble to the peace
That was among them...
Nor less in springtime when on southern banks
The shining sun had from his knot of leaves
Decoy'd the primrose flower, and when the Vales
And woods were warm, was I a plunderer then
In the high places, on the lonesome peaks
Where'er, among the mountains and the winds,
The mother bird had built her lodge. Though mean
My object, and inglorious, yet the end
Was not ignoble. Oh! when I have hung
Above the raven's nest, by knots of grass
And half-inch fissures in the slippery rock
But ill sustain'd, and almost, as it seem'd
Suspended by the blast which blew amain,
Shouldering the naked crag; Oh! at that time
While on the perilous ridge I hung alone,
With what strange utterance did the loud dry wind
Blow through my ears! the sky seem'd not a sky
Of earth, and with what motion mov'd the clouds!

WILLIAM WORDSWORTH

*traps

Revisiting No. 33

Her home was up a clutter of stairs,
a twist of darkness, where the tap tap
of her stick tipped your spine.
Black skirts. Black shawl.
Fingers like heather roots.

The wind lists now at the glass,
unpicks the paint, scatters cherry blossom
from the trees folk used to say
should have been rowans,
and there's nothing there to show
the shiver of air
that hung around her door
– those clenched-heart dares
to ring her bell and run away.

It was said she never ate, it was said
she ate the dust, it was said
she smothered children,
it was said she knew the small talk
of the moon – so many words
chased us along the street
till we'd hurtle in a heap
behind a hedge
and believe
and not believe each other.

DOROTHY BAIRD

The Boy's Song

Where the pools are bright and deep,
Where the grey trout lies asleep,
Up the river and o'er the lea –
That's the way for Billy and me.

Where the blackbird sings the latest,
Where the hawthorn blooms the sweetest,
Where the nestlings chirp and flee –
That's the way for Billy and me.

Where the mowers mow the cleanest,
Where the hay lies thick and greenest,
There to trace the homeward bee –
That's the way for Billy and me.

Where the hazel bank is steepest,
Where the shadow falls the deepest,
Where the clustering nuts fall free –
That's the way for Billy and me.

There let us walk, there let us play,
Through the meadows, among the hay,
Up the water, and o'er the lea –
That's the way for Billy and me.

JAMES HOGG

The Schoolboy

I love to rise in a summer morn
When the birds sing on every tree;
The distant huntsman winds his horn,
And the sky-lark sings with me.
O! what sweet company.

But to go to school in a summer morn,
O! it drives all joy away;
Under a cruel eye outworn,
The little ones spend the day
In sighing and dismay.

Ah! then at times I drooping sit,
And spend many an anxious hour,
Nor in my book can I take delight,
Nor sit in learning's bower,
Worn thro' with the dreary shower.

How can the bird that is born for joy
Sit in a cage and sing?
How can a child, when fears annoy,
But droop his tender wing,
And forget his youthful spring?

O! father and mother, if buds are nipp'd
And blossoms blown away,
And if the tender plants are stripp'd
Of their joy in the springing day,
By sorrow and care's dismay,

How shall the summer arise in joy,
Or the summer fruits appear?
Or how shall we gather what griefs destroy,
Or bless the mellowing year,
When the blasts of winter appear?

WILLIAM BLAKE

The Land of Counterpane

When I was sick and lay a-bed,
I had two pillows at my head,
And all my toys beside me lay
To keep me happy all the day.

And sometimes for an hour or so
I watched my leaden soldiers go,
With different uniforms and drills,
Among the bed-clothes, through the hills;

And sometimes sent my ships in fleets
All up and down among the sheets;
Or brought my trees and houses out,
And planted cities all about.

I was the giant great and still
That sits upon the pillow hill,
And sees before him, dale and plain,
The pleasant land of counterpane.

ROBERT LOUIS STEVENSON

Mama's Magic

My Mama is Magic!
Always was and always will be.
There is one phrase that constantly bubbled
from the lips of her five children, "My momma can do it."
We thought my momma knew everything.
Believed she did, as if she were born full grown from the
                              Encyclopedia Britannica.
I could tell you stories.
How she transformed a run down paint peeled shack into a home.
How she heated us with tin tub baths from a kettle on a stove.
Poured it over in there like an elixir.

We were my mama's favorite recipe.
She whipped us up from a big brown bowl, supported by her big
                              brown arms.
We were homemade children.
Stitched together with homemade love.
We didn't get everything we ever wanted
but lacked for nothing.

My mama's was protection!
Like those quilts her mother used to make.
She tucked us in with patches of cut out history all around us.
We found we could walk anywhere in this world and not feel alone.

My mama never whispered the shame of poverty in our ears.
She taught us to dance to our own shadows.
Pay no attention to those grand parties on the other side of the track.
Make your own music she'd say
as she walked, as she cleaned
the sagging floorboards of that place.
You'll get there. You'll get there.

Her broom seemed to say with every wisp.
We looked at the stars in my mama's eyes, they told us we owned
$$\text{the world.}$$
We walked like kings and queens even on midnight trips to the
outhouse.
We were under her spell. My mama didn't study at no Harvard or
no Yale.
but the things she knew
you couldn't learn in no book!
Like......
how to make your life sing like sweet potato pie sweetness
out of an open window.
How to make anybody feel at home.
How at just the right moment be silent,
be silent, then with her eyes say, "Everything's gonna be alright,
$$\text{chile,}$$
everything is gonna be alright."
How she tended to our sickness.
How she raised our spirits.
How she kept flowers living on our dilapidated porch in the midst of
family chaos.
My mama raised children like it was her business in life.
Put us on her hip and kept moving.
Keeping that house Pine-sol clean.
Yeah, my mama is magic. Always was and always will be.
Her magic. How to stay steady and sure in this fast pace world
Now when people look at me
with my head held high.
My back erect and say
Who does she think she is?
I just keep walking
with the assurance inside.
I am Black Magic.
And I am Jeanette Redmond's child.

GLENIS REDMOND

Recipe for a Mother

Take one heart and stretch it
until it can withstand laughter
and tears in vast measures
at the same time.

Add a liberal dollop of patience,
bind with a strong sense of humour
and marinade
for at least 18 years.

Scatter a fine disregard
for dirty washing, untidy bedrooms
and all cutting comments, particularly those
made by teenagers.

Chop up several pounds of personal aims
and set aside for a minimum of 12 years.
Add an extra pair of hands, a blind eye, and a deaf ear,
to use as needed – and zest
and spice of your choice.

Arrange in a dish with a good helping
of women friends. Ensure the centre
still holds its shape even if circumstances
threaten to dissolve it.

Put in a warm house. Make sure this
is big enough to allow for
exponentially increasing clutter.

Bake through long afternoons
of playing shops, pushing swings, monopoly,

girl/boyfriend worries, acne and exams.
Keep baking at night, weekends and holidays.

Turn out just when things become smoother. If
it sinks, decorate with fresh interests. Use
nostalgia sparingly … It's not done yet –
and there are no accolades for your skill,
but still – remember to
sit back a moment in the sun
– and enjoy …

DOROTHY BAIRD

Their Father

They leap to him,
the little one all leggy
and the elder, with her Iseult heart
that knows a knight when it sees one.

He is the kite-rigger
and the armoured escort;
he sees a route past the impasse.

After supper
they learn chess from him
and almost win.

He sanctifies routine:
he is a kingdom
that is not yet built.

GABRIEL MILLAR

The Children's Hour

Between the dark and the daylight,
When the night is beginning to lower,
Comes a pause in the day's occupations,
That is known as the Children's Hour.

I hear in the chamber above me
The patter of little feet,
The sound of a door that is opened,
And voices soft and sweet.

From my study I see in the lamplight,
Descending the broad hall stair,
Grave Alice and laughing Allegra,
And Edith with golden hair.

A whisper and then a silence:
Yet I know by their merry eyes
They are plotting and planning together
To take me by surprise.

A sudden rush from the stairway,
A sudden raid from the hall!
By three doors left unguarded
They enter my castle wall!

They climb up into my turret
O'er the arms and back of my chair;
If I try to escape, they surround me;
They seem to be everywhere.

They almost devour me with kisses,
Their arms about me entwine,

Till I think of the Bishop of Bingen
In his Mouse-Tower on the Rhine!

Do you think, O blue-eyed banditti,
Because you have scaled the wall,
Such an old mustache as I am
Is not a match for you all?

I have you fast in my fortress,
And will not let you depart,
But put you down into the dungeon
In the round-tower of my heart.

And there I will keep you forever,
Yes, forever and a day,
Till the walls shall crumble to ruin,
And moulder in dust away!

HENRY WADSWORTH LONGFELLOW

Schoolboys in Winter

The schoolboys still their morning rambles take
To neighbouring village schools with playing speed,
Loitering with pastime's leisure till they quake,
Oft looking up the wild-geese droves to heed,
Watching the letters which their journeys make;
Or plucking haws on which the fieldfares feed,
And hips and sloes! and on each shallow lake
Making glib slides, where they like shadows go
Till some fresh pastimes in their minds awake.
Then off they start anew and hasty blow
Their numbed and clumpsing fingers till they glow;
Then races with their shadows wildly run
That stride huge giants o'er the shining snow
In the pale splendour of the winter sun.

John Clare

From The Prelude

And in the frosty season, when the sun
Was set, and visible for many a mile
The cottage windows through the twilight blazed,
I heeded not the summons: happy time
It was indeed for all of us – to me
It was a time of rapture! Clear and loud
The village clock tolled six, – I wheeled about,

Proud and exultant like an untired horse
That cares not for its home. All shod with steel,
We hissed along the polished ice in games
Confederate, imitative of the chase
And woodland pleasures, – the resounding horn,
The pack loud bellowing, and the hunted hare,
So through the darkness and the cold we flew,
And not a voice was idle; with the din,
Meanwhile, the precipices rang aloud;
The leafless trees and every icy crag
Tinkled like iron; while the distant hills
Into the tumult sent an alien sound
Of melancholy not unnoticed, while the stars
Eastward were sparkling clear, and in the west
The orange sky of evening died away.
Not seldom from the uproar I retired
Into a silent bay or sportively
Glanced sideway, leaving the tumultuous throng,
To cut across the image of a star
That gleamed upon the ice; and oftentimes,
When we had given our bodies to the wind,
And all the shadowy banks on either side
Came sweeping through the darkness, spinning still
The rapid line of motion, then at once
Have I reclining back upon my heels,
Stopped short; yet still the solitary cliffs
Wheeled by me – even as if the earth had rolled
With visible motion her diurnal round!
Behind me did they stretch in solemn train,
Feebler and feebler, and I stood and watched
Till all was tranquil as a dreamless sleep.

WILLIAM WORDSWORTH

SORROW'S SPRINGS: ILLNESS AND UPSET

The poems in this section touch on illness, grief and fear of both parents and children. Without overlooking the reality of pain, they soften it with understanding and by giving it expression.

Spring and Fall

To a young child

Márgarét, áre you gríeving
Over Goldengrove unleaving?
Leáves, like the things of man, you
With your fresh thoughts care for, can you?
Áh! ás the heart grows older
It will come to such sights colder
By and by, nor spare a sigh
Though worlds of wanwood leafmeal lie;
And yet you *will* weep and know why.
Now no matter, child, the name:
Sórrow's springs áre the same.
Nor mouth had, no nor mind, expressed
What heart heard of, ghost guessed:
It ís the blight man was born for,
It is Margaret you mourn for.

GERARD MANLEY HOPKINS

Crib Song

The baby lies inside her crib.
This night is made of
        strange imaginings, bent twice

        around my mind.
Is marriage over now
that we don't speak
                but through good friends convey
demands:
        your drugs, my past, our daughter's life?

The baby lies inside her crib,
                        too small

    to feel
        the anger (we hope)   in the air between

        our separate worlds,
                her skin so soft all things

        afraid to harm her veer away, these words,
                        this rage, her parents we are
                failing to
become.
I am afraid to touch her face, Imago made of what we made, let go.

                But she just smiles,
                her chin tucked down toward
                her heart.

The last thing in the world

                to break in three.

LAURA HOPE-GILL

The Poet and the Toddler

He likes to ride on my shoulders
Ethan does
because he says it makes him tall.
Taller than even the grown ups he says.
This child
the father of the man
riding his grown up,
I feel I am a gawky half a horse.

The child who jockies me,
when he was only two weeks old,
was limp as death, his soft flesh cold,
his new eyes glazed by cataracts of waning
life.
And after a frantic dance of doctors' gowns
and parental panic, spinal taps, and PIC lines
his tiny limbs and fragile chest
became the hub of a tangled array of tubes,
wires, and machines
But he chose to stay
and die another day.

You'll see him everywhere
if you only look:

A green shock of leaves
on a tree stump
left for dead.

The weed that breaks
the sidewalk's surface
grasping at the sun.

A lone ant lugging a crumb.

You'll see him everywhere:

The small fighter
with his pockets full of rocks.

The scrapper with an instinct
for a miracle.

Now he sits taller than grown ups.
Now he is pulling my hair.
Covering my eyes.
Removing my glasses.
Sticking his fingers in my ears.

God
looking down must wonder at the sight
and rifle through his notes
to discover the name of this creature
the one that looks like an awkward stalk of wheat.

Ah, here it is, God says,
as he looks into the index
of His book of Divine Inspiration.
One of my greatest inventions:

The Poet and the Toddler

the deep well
holding on its shoulder
        the necessary bucket.

ALLAN WOLF

The Sick Child

She breathes with mouse breath,
a faint fustiness drifting from her lips.
We sit, watching blue-tits on the nuts,
lulled by the syncopated rise

of lungs. She is a rag-doll in my lap,
head under chin, hands dangling,
empty of the fizz that fires her
into endless moving.

A car passes. The sun strolls
beyond the window. She leans
against me, curving to fit
my hollows and I would grow

another skin, to wrap her in
my darkness
till she's ready again
to push towards the light.

DOROTHY BAIRD

The Sick Child

Child: O Mother, lay your hand on my brow!
O mother, mother, where am I now?
Why is the room so gaunt and great?
Why am I lying awake so late?

Mother: Fear not at all: the night is still.
Nothing is here that means you ill –
Nothing but lamps the whole town through,
And never a child awake but you.

Child: Mother, mother, speak low in my ear,
Some of the things are so great and near,
Some are so small and far away,
I have a fear that I cannot say.
What have I done, and what do I fear,
And why are you crying, mother dear?

Mother: Out in the city sounds begin.
Thank the kind God, the carts come in!
An hour or two more, and God is so kind,
The day shall be blue in the window blind,
Then shall my child go sweetly asleep,
And dream of the birds and the hills of sheep.

ROBERT LOUIS STEVENSON

Bedtime

Dad suck my nightmare out he said
I think I've got one coming in my head.
All right I paused
crossed to his bed & kneeling
rested my mouth upon his waiting ear and
gulped it out.
Now the other one he said.
No gulp a second time   more
a sip. There wasn't much left I said. Tonight
you'll be all right.
You sure? He snuggling said. Oh yes
I'm sure.
I woke a short sleep later   eased
My body from his floor and room.

Do you think he asked me once
we'll still kiss ears when I'm grown up?
You never know your luck
I smiling said.

JEREMY MULFORD

The Shoes

These are the shoes
Dad walked about in
when we did jobs
in the garden,

when his shed
was full of shavings,
when he tried to put the fence up,
when my old bike
needed mending,
when the car
could not get started,
when he got up late
on Sunday.
These are the shoes
Dad walked about in
and I've kept them
in my room.

These are not the shoes
that Dad walked out in
when we didn't know where he was going,
when I tried to lift
his suitcase,
when he said goodbye
and kissed me,
when he left his door-key
on the table,
when he promised Mum
he'd send a postcard,
when I couldn't hear
his special footsteps.
These are not the shoes
that Dad walked out in
but he'll need them
when he comes home.

JOHN MOLE

Return Journeys

The day had been as good
as I might have hoped and so
I resisting sadness said goodbye
a few times with as many kisses
and drove the car away.

I noted the miles not wanting
to see the city's sameness greet me,
the quite ordinary encroachments of its outer reaches
& accumulating side streets of
the last stretch home.

When. Lo. Twelve miles before the city a reprieve
greeted with a curse of course –
my handy carrier no less
I'd left behind.

Handy indeed –
no option but to turn
and with another *sotto* curse
gleefully drive back
return
to a jolly reunion – such
a surprise for everyone.

Everyone seemed pleased
though dutifully they said how sorry they were
for me and I
dutifully agreed, then told them I was pleased.
More kisses from my children
& hugs – even
a cheese sandwich from their mother.

Odd how cheerful
the second drive was made by this –
how welcome the darkness
of this second journey toward
those outer reaches
those side streets.
That way home.

JEREMY MULFORD

Sleeping with Amy

Sleeping with you   I want
nothing   but the cheek by cheek
sharing of the in and out
breath of our three years
your curls around my fingers

ball-curled   filling the void
between my thigh and chin
you ask nothing   but the warm
press of flesh   a shell
against the darkness of your dreams

GILLIE GRIFFIN

From Psalm 22

Be not far from me, for trouble is near, for there is none to help…
I am poured out like water, and all my bones are out of joint: my heart
is like wax; it is melted in the midst of my bowels…My strength is
dried up like a potsherd; and my tongue cleaveth to my jaws; and thou
hast brought me into the dust of death…But be thou not far from me,
O Lord: O my strength, haste thee to help me.

From Affliction IV

Broken in pieces all asunder
Lord, hunt me not,
A thing forgot,
My thoughts are all a case of knives,
Wounding my heart
With scattered smart.

GEORGE HERBERT

From Carrion Comfort

My own heart let me more have pity on; let
Me live to my sad self hereafter kind,
Charitable; not live this tormented mind
With this tormenting mind tormenting yet.
       I cast for comfort I can no more get
By groping round my comfortless, than blind
Eyes in their dark can day or thirst can find
Thirst's all-in-all in all a world of wet.

Soul, self; come, poor Jackself, I do advise
You, jaded, let be; call off thoughts awhile
Elsewhere; leave comfort root-room; let joy size
At God knows when to God knows what; whose smile
's not wrung, see you; unforeseen times rather – as skies
betweenpie mountains – lights a lovely mile.

GERARD MANLEY HOPKINS

From The Wreck of the Deutschland

Thou mastering me
God! Giver of breath and bread;
World's strand, sway of the sea;
Lord of living and dead;
Thou hast bound bones and veins in me, fastened me flesh,
And after it almost unmade, what with dread,
Thy doing: and dost thou touch me afresh?
Over again I feel thy finger and find thee.

GERARD MANLEY HOPKINS

One, Two, Whatever You Do

One, two, whatever you do,
Start it well and carry it through;
Try, try, never say die,
Things will come right, you know, by and by.

ANON

A WIND WHERE THE ROSE WAS: BEREAVEMENT

Death is something young children don't understand. A friend once recalled how, as a four-year-old, she found a dead bird and couldn't understand why it wouldn't fly: she picked it up and tried to make its wings flap! Perhaps though, young children's failure to understand death is a greater understanding than our so-called understanding. Perhaps death is less real to them because instinctively they know life doesn't end (see the poem by Wordsworth in this section)…

But for us adults there can be little worse, more wrong-seeming, than the death of a child, the premature end before life's properly begun, before the individual promise each child brings has unfolded.

The poems below try to deal in different ways with death, from both child and adult perspectives.

Janet Waking

Beautifully Janet slept
Till it was deeply morning. She woke then
And thought about her dainty-feathered hen,
To see how it had kept.

One kiss she gave her mother
Only a small one she gave to her daddy
Who would have kissed each curl of his shining baby;
No kiss at all for her brother.

'Old Chucky, Old Chucky!' she cried,
running across the world upon the grass
to Chucky's house, and listening. But alas,
her Chucky had died.

It was a transmogrifying bee
Came droning down on Chucky's old bald head
And sat and put the poison. It scarcely bled,
But how exceedingly

And purply did the knot
Swell with the venom and communicate
Its rigor! Now the poor comb stood up straight
But Chucky did not.

So there was Janet
Kneeling on the wet grass, crying her brown hen
(Translated far beyond the daughters of men)
To rise and walk upon it.

And weeping fast as she had breath
Janet implored us, 'Wake her from sleep!'
And would not be instructed in how deep
Was the forgetful kingdom of death.

JOHN CROWE RANSOM

Russet Leaves

Russet leaves! Russet leaves! Triumphant on high,
Touched by the crimson summer's sky,
Embers aloft, as the dragon's wide eye,
Russet leaves, fear you, fear you to die?

Nay child! Nay child! To die fear we never,
We fear neither besom, nor blast of the weather;
We rejoice when the scowling squall snips our frail tether:
Nay child! We'll pelter down, pelter together.

Russet leaves! Russet leaves! Stout oak's trumpet choir,
Shrink you not from the clay and the dung of the byre,
To be muted and choked in the smouldering fire;
Russet leaves will you bow, bow deep as the mire?

Yea child! Yea child! We'll gladly be tossed,
And rotted and ditched, or crunched by Jack Frost,
Or sandwiched 'twixt layers of kitchen compost:
Spring's green voice will proclaim:
                                   We never are lost!

BRIEN MASTERS

From We Are Seven

– A simple Child,
That lightly draws its breath,
And feels its life in every limb,
What should it know of death?

I met a little cottage Girl:
She was eight years old, she said;
Her hair was thick with many a curl
That clustered round her head.

She had a rustic, woodland air,
And she was wildly clad:
Her eyes were fair and very fair;
- Her beauty made me glad.

"Sisters and brothers, little Maid,
How many may you be?"
"How many? Seven in all," she said,
And wondering looked at me.

"And where are they? I pray you tell."
She answered, "Seven are we;
And two of us at Conway dwell
And two are gone to sea.

"Two of us in the church-yard lie,
My sister and my brother;
And, in the church-yard cottage, I
Dwell near them with my mother."

You say that two at Conway dwell,
And two are gone to sea,
Yet ye are seven! I pray you tell,
Sweet maid, how this may be."

Then did the little Maid reply,
"Seven boys and girls are we;
Two of us in the church-yard lie,
Beneath the church-yard tree."

"You run about, my little Maid,
Your limbs they are alive;
If two are in the church-yard laid
Then ye are only five."

"Their graves are green, they may be seen,"
The little Maid replied,
"Twelve steps or more from my mother's door
and they are side by side.

"My stockings there I often knit,
my kerchief there I hem;
and there upon the ground I sit,
and sing a song for them..."

..."How many are you, then," said I,
If they two are in heaven?"
Quick was the little Maid's reply,
"O Master! we are seven...."

WILLIAM WORDSWORTH

The Land of Dreams

Awake, awake, my little Boy!
Thou wast thy Mother's only joy;
Why dost thou weep in thy gentle sleep?
Awake! thy Father does thee keep.

'O, what Land is the Land of Dreams?
What are its Mountains & what are its Streams?
O Father, I saw my Mother there,
Among the lilies by waters fair.

'Among the Lambs, clothed in white,
she walk'd with her Thomas in sweet delight.
I wept for joy, like a dove I mourn;
O! when shall I again return?'

Dear Child, I also by pleasant Streams
Have wander'd all Night in the Land of Dreams;
But tho' calm & warm the waters wide,
I could not get to the other side.

'Father, O Father! what do we here
in this Land of unbelief & fear?
The Land of Dreams is better far,
Above the light of the Morning Star.'

WILLIAM BLAKE

The Dead Girl

They think that I am dead,
All weeping by the bed.

But through the window come the sounds of Spring –
The first shy cuckoo, faint but clear:
The bubbling water of the rain-filled stream
I know is rushing by the weir.

And I am weary of this darkened room,
The stealthy sobs, the stuffy heat;
Beyond the window are the things I love –
Like fieldmice in the green young wheat.

Farewell then, and God bless you, for I go
Out through the window, like a sprite:
Out from this dark enclosing cell of flesh
Into the freedom and the light.

(They think that I am dead,
All weeping by the bed!)

CATHERINE PETERS
WRITTEN WHEN THE AUTHOR WAS 12

Drowning

Gazing at the enormous sun I promise
to ask for nothing again ever
if his life is saved. They pump out water,
breathe down into him,
but I see his eyes turn over...

they send me on some excuse of an errand
across the sand. I stagger off
and back in a bright blindness, forgetting why
I've been sent, heavy with the hollow
stone of hidden love that weighs
up out of my stomach.

Then waiting for the miracle. Trying to disbelieve,
as it goes by, the black car's sign –
friends try to hold me, I run
all the way back up the road: they're loading him in.

An Irishman cradles my head in his hands –
O those hands, bless them, but I run again
into my mother's embrace at the door of the house –
where my memory fades, loss into loss...

But I remember how
she climbs between the sheets he slept in
only the night before, when alive;
vanishes under the unbearable
hill of silence, seeking him.
And where is he? What last rending
union does she find?

Or does only absence numb
her sleeplessness? The rain
rattles down darkness all night in my room.

MATTHEW BARTON

That's Normal

If you think you're going insane –
that's normal.

If all you do is cry –
that's normal.

If you can't make any kind of decision –
that's normal.

If your food tastes like dust –
that's normal.

If you feel rage, denial and depression –
that's normal.

If you find yourself enjoying a funny moment and immediately feel
guilty –
that's normal.

If your friends dwindle away and you feel like you have the plague –
that's normal.

If your blood boils and the hairs in your nose curl when someone tells you it's God's will –
that's normal.

If you can't talk about it but you can smash dishes, shred old phone books or kick the garbage can (preferably empty) down the street –
that's normal.

If you can share your feelings with an understanding listener, another bereaved person –
that's a beginning.

If you can get a glimmer of your child's or partner's life, rather than death –
that's wonderful.

If you can remember your child or partner's smile –
that's healing.

If you can find your mirrors have become windows and you are able to reach out to other bereaved people –
that's growing.

ANON

Autumn

There is a wind where the rose was;
Cold rain where sweet grass was;
    And clouds like sheep
    Stream o'er the steep
Grey skies where the lark was.

Nought gold where your hair was;
Nought warm where your hand was;
    But phantom, forlorn,
    Beneath the thorn,
Your ghost where your face was.

Sad winds where your voice was;
Tears, tears where my heart was;
    And ever with me,
    Child, ever with me,
Silence where hope was.

WALTER DE LA MARE

On My First Son

Farewell, thou child of my right hand and joy;
    My sin was too much hope of thee, loved boy,
Seven years thou wert lent to me, and I thee pay,
    Exacted by thy fate, on the just day.
O, could I lose all father, now. For why
    Will man lament the state he should envy?
To have so soon 'scaped worlds, and flesh's rage,
    And, if no other misery, yet age?
Rest in soft peace, and, asked, say here doth lie
    Ben Jonson his best piece of poetry:
For whose sake, henceforth, all his vows be such,
    As what he loves may never like too much.

BEN JONSON

The Elf King

Who rides so late where winds blow wild?
A father tightly grasping his child.
He holds the boy embraced in his arm,
Clasping him to him, keeping him warm.

'My son, why cover your face in such fear?'
'Father, do you see the elf-king come near?
The king of the elves with crown and train!'
'My son, it's just mist upon the plain.'

'Sweet lad, O come and join me, do!
Such pretty games I'll play with you;
On the shore fair flowers their colours unfold,
My mother has garments of silver and gold.'

'My father, my father, and can you not hear
the promise the elf-king breathes in my ear?'
'Be calm, stay calm, my child, lie low:
In old withered leaves the night winds blow.'

'Sweet lad, come closer, come with me -
My daughters shall care for you tenderly;
My daughters their nightly revelry keep,
They'll rock you and dance you and sing you to sleep.'

'My father, my father, O do you not see
the elf-king's daughters beckoning me?'
'My son, my son, I see quite clear
just ancient willows bending here.'

'I love you, your comeliness charms me my boy!
And if you're not willing, my force I'll employ.'
'Now father, now father, he seizes my arm:
the elf-king has done me a cruel harm.'

The father shudders, his horse gallops on
In his arms he holds his groaning son,
He reaches the courtyard in panic and dread –
The child he holds in his arms is dead.

JOHANN WOLFGANG VON GOETHE

In Painswick Churchyard

'Is this where people are buried?
I will not let them bury you'

He picnics among tombs
– pours imaginary tea,
a yew tree his kitchen

'You will live with me in my house'

Oh could I believe the living and the dead inhabit one house under
the sky and you my child run into your future for ever

FRANCES HOROVITZ

From Melodious One of the Mountains

Thou art my precious Lord,
Thou art my strong pillar,
Thou art the sustenance of my breast:
Oh part thou from me never!

For mine afflictions forsake me not,
For my tears' sake do not leave me!
Jesu! Thou likeness of the sun,
In the day of my need be near me!

Thou great Lord of the sun,
In the day of my need be near me;
Thou great being of the universe,
Keep me in the surety of thine arms!

Leave me not in dumbness,
Dead in the wilderness;
Leave me not to my stumbling,
For my trust in thee, my Saviour!

Though I had no fire,
Thy warmth did not fail me;
Though I had no clothing,
Thy love did not forsake me.

Though I had no hearth,
The cold did not numb me;
Though I knew not the ways,
Thy knowledge was around me […]

Though the stones were diamonds,
Though they were dollars of gold,
Though the whole ocean were wine,
Offered to me of right;

Though the earth were cinnamon
And the lakes were of honey,
Dearer were a vision of Christ
In peace, in love, in pity.

Jesu, meet thou my soul!
Jesu, clothe me in thy love!
Jesu shield thou my spirit!
Jesu stretch out to me thine hand!

ANON
TRANSLATED FROM THE GAELIC BY
ALEXANDER CARMICHAEL

For you, Papa

I thought I heard your footsteps
Running towards me
Disturbing the stones.
But when I opened my eyes,
I saw it was only the waves,
Pulling and swirling like hands.
I thought I felt your smile,
Warm and loving upon my face.
But when I opened my eyes,
I saw it was only the sun,
Beaming at me from across the water.

I thought I heard you
Whisper my name.
But when I opened my eyes,
I realized it was only the wind
Playing in my hair.

I thought I felt you
Softly kiss my cheek.
But when I opened my eyes,
I saw it was only a leaf
Caressing me with gentle strokes.

And then I felt your love
In and all around me.
Powerful yet gentle like the waves,
Warm and shining like the sun,
Soft yet strong like the wind,
Tender and alive like the leaves.
And I didn't even have
To open my eyes.
I knew you were there.

KIRSTEN BERGH, AGED 17

Remembering Anna

The wall rebuilt in neat, new brick.
Beyond it the same straggle of bush
where she lay freshly dead a year back: sent
headlong by a car from joke, chat, can
of drink to what she couldn't place –
lesson too fast to learn, life reeling off
to rattling seedhead, spool of lost
body's buds, its leaves and scents.
       A year on I
– not knowing it's a year – pass, find
fresh flowers laid here in their films
of cellophane; drawings, cards
To Anna, messages sealed
for her deep-sealed eyes alone, from kids
who climbed back into daylight – yet keep on
turning to the place a death's
pull draws them to, hold hands, talk, laugh,
light candles, post their love beyond
what's visible – knowing that she's gone
deep into them where hurt is
hand-in-glove with open heart.

MATTHEW BARTON

Said by the father of a child who died at birth:

The life she did not live has become our inner life

From Adonais

XL

He has outsoared the shadow of our night;
Envy and calumny, and hate and pain,
And that unrest which men miscall delight,
Can touch him not and torture not again;
From the contagion of the world's slow stain
He is secure, and now can never mourn
A heart grown cold, a head grown grey in vain;
Nor when the spirit's self has ceased to burn
With sparkless ashes load an unlamented urn.

XLI

He lives, he wakes – 'tis Death is dead, not he;
Mourn not for Adonais. – Thou young Dawn,
Turn all thy dew to splendour, for from thee
The spirit thou lamentest is not gone;
Ye caverns and ye forests, cease to moan!
Cease, ye faint flowers and fountains, and thou Air
Which like a mourning veil thy scarf hadst thrown
O'er the abandoned Earth, now leave it bare
Even to the joyous stars which smile on its despair!

XLII

He is made one with Nature: there is heard
His voice in all her music, from the moan
Of thunder, to the song of night's sweet bird;
He is a presence to be felt and known
In darkness and in light, from herb and stone,
Spreading itself where'er that Power may move
Which has withdrawn his being to its own;
Which wields the world with never-wearied love,
Sustains it from beneath and kindles it above.

PERCY BYSSHE SHELLEY

'Do not stand at my grave and weep'

Do not stand at my grave and weep;
I am not there. I do not sleep.
I am a thousand winds that blow.
I am the diamond glints on snow.
I am the sunlight on ripened grain.
I am the gentle autumn rain.
When you awaken in the morning's hush
I am the swift uplifting rush
Of quiet birds in circled flight.
I am the soft stars that shine at night.
Do not stand at my grave and cry;
I am not there. I did not die.

Anon
*(Said to have been written to his parents by
a solder in World War I)*

From For Now

For my mother

You came in light
You were waiting for me;
You came into my body
I only knew you as you left –

Knew it was you now
As light as you were, then
As you opened my heart in your going
As you said:

'Only be the brightness of what you are.'

Jay Ramsay

The Swan

Tied up in clumsy knots we live: laborious
clambering through all that's still not done yet, like
the swan's ungainly, awkward gait.

But dying we lose grasp
of daily ground we clung to –
the tentative way the swan lowers himself

into waters which embrace him
glide away under him, light as breathing,
pour on easily and flow -
while endlessly serene and still,
with growing assurance, ever more
sovereign mastery he sweeps on.

RAINER MARIA RILKE
TRANSLATED BY MATTHEW BARTON

Verse

No boundaries separate
where spirit links sustain
light-brilliant,
love-radiant
eternal soul bonds.

So I am in your thoughts,
so you in mine.

RUDOLF STEINER

PART IV

THE GROUND TO STAND ON: STEPPING OUT AND GROWING AWAY

The poems which follow are all in some way connected with the long journey into distinct, separate selfhood: from the first realisation that we are alone to the self-assertion of adolescence and early adulthood. From the age of 9 or so, children often start to feel a new and painful separation from those around them, questioning things they had taken for granted. This grows into rebellion and also, hopefully, confirmation in the widest sense of who they are, their aims, hopes and direction.

My parents

They gave me life
Can it be that what I am
Is theirs?
They cannot know my thoughts and hopes
And fears.

They gave me life,
Yet all I am is mine
Not theirs.
I've lived within my self alone
For years.

They gave me life
To run and think and grow my way
Not theirs.
Now can I give them my happiness
Not tears.

MARK VINTEN, AGED 10

On Turning Ten

The whole idea of it makes me feel
like I'm coming down with something,
something worse than any stomach ache
or the headaches I get from reading in bad light –
a kind of measles of the spirit,
a mumps of the psyche,
a disfiguring chicken pox of the soul.

You tell me it is too early to be looking back,
but that is because you have forgotten
the perfect simplicity of being one
and the beautiful complexity introduced by two.
But I can lie on my bed and remember every digit.
At four I was an Arabian wizard.
I could make myself invisible
by drinking a glass of milk a certain way.
At seven I was a soldier, at nine a prince.

But now I am mostly at the window
watching the late afternoon light.
Back then it never fell so solemnly
against the side of my tree house,
and my bicycle never leaned against the garage
as it does today,
all the dark blue speed drained out of it.

This is the beginning of sadness, I say to myself,
as I walk through the universe in my sneakers.
It is time to say good-bye to my imaginary friends,
time to turn the first big number.

It seems only yesterday I used to believe
there was nothing under my skin but light.
If you cut me I could shine.
But now when I fall upon the sidewalks of life,
I skin my knees. I bleed.

BILLY COLLINS

Learning To Row

Not quite closing the ring
round the oar-shafts, she takes the strain:
you in the prow, me in the stern;
her hands nearly knit, nearly heal
in a heartbeat as they meet
for a moment then push
off from each other like negative poles.

Later when she's learnt
this balancing act,
we let her go. She calls
back from far out:

It's much easier on my own…

And again and again
lifts clear from the broken
reflection her whole
undreamed depth of wings.

MATTHEW BARTON

Fall

The old apple tree opens
its moth-eaten parachute over you,
ten years old, twilighting on ropes,
swinging, slipping
into your limbs.

We're lying beneath.
in the half light it seems
life's rushing up to meet you, starting
to weigh the apples of your eyes.

And I wonder:
can we bless
and rein your fall
with gentleness?

MATTHEW BARTON

Letting Go

In his bag a warm drink and a torch
he wasn't asked to bring.
The weight of the cold phone
in my hand is a measure
of the distance between us. *Aw Mum
I won't need that*
                            as he eases himself
into the thicket of boys, while I stand
and watch them diminished
by the hills and the night.
Ocht they'll be fine out there
in the sweep of the stars and the rocks
and all the empty dark

– won't they?

DOROTHY BAIRD

Relief

A blue afternoon in August.
They slip from a familiar shape
to a space, where all that is, is their absence.

Black-headed gulls squawk
over a yoghurt carton.
A woman, whose grey hair is long
as an old mermaid, leans

into the shelter
of her man's thick jumper.
Water laps against the jetty.

I imagine their paddles
turning like windmills, the boat
bumping against waves, water
the colour of a bruise, lifted into light
that trails down arms. Her eyes
will be furrowed with determination.

She is only eight.

The bench hardens. A wind picks up.
The woman's hair wafts like seaweed
Against the shoulder of a rock.
My watch is barely moving. But
I'm well behaved, sip cups of tea, until
the sea has swallowed them
and the afternoon's turned black.

And then the headland
gifts them back, paddles
scything the air. 'Seals'
she sings, 'out there,
so close we heard them breathe!'

The mermaid smiles
As if she understands.
I press my palms,
sooth out the nail marks
buried in my hands.

DOROTHY BAIRD

Middle of the Road

For the boys

The game that ended in an explosive
ball intentionally chucked way over
the top, and turned
into a hurl of words instead –

carries on in the car:
back and forth they lob the ins and outs,
reaching past reason into
the voluble absolute.

I keep my eyes on the road; for once
don't want to fault them, suddenly know they're miles
truer than my tortuous attempts
to please and appease. They're right there getting stuck in

to themselves up to the ears: deaf
to anything but the deepening
pitch of their own voices sounding them
with presence like pitchers filling with new wine.

MATTHEW BARTON

A Confirmation
For Thel

A rainstorm shook the window
when you were born,
but today on your Confirmation
even you might
pausing a moment say
how strange to be this girl I am
under the Flowering Cherry.

A stone is firm.
A purpose in the mind
is firm.
But how can a gust like you
find confirmation   unless
under the flowering tree
you pause
and in the stillness find
God's ground to stand on.

PAUL MATTHEWS

My soul: your wishes bud
My will: your deeds flourish
My life: your fruits ripen.

I feel my destiny,
My destiny finds me.
I feel my star,
My star finds me.
I feel my aims,
My aims find me.

My soul and the world are but one.

Life, you grow brighter around me,
Life you grow harder for me,
Life you grow richer within me.

RUDOLF STEINER

Vigour shine through me
strength sing through me,
shine and sing
through legs and arms,
sing and shine
through hands and feet:
so I will grow vigorous,
will grow strong
in heart and head,
vigorous and strong
in breath and speech.

RUDOLF STEINER

Poem for a Rite of Passage

In beauty	may I walk
All day long	may I walk
Through the returning seasons	may I walk
Beautifully will I possess again	
Beautifully birds	
Beautifully joyful birds	
On the trail marked with pollen	may I walk
With grasshoppers about my feet	may I walk
With dew about my feet	may I walk
With beauty	may I walk
With beauty before me	may I walk
With beauty behind me	may I walk
With beauty above me	may I walk
With beauty all around me	may I walk
In old age, wandering on a trail of beauty, lively,	may I walk
In old age, wandering on a trail of beauty, living again,	may I walk
It is finished in beauty	
It is finished in beauty	

ANON

TRANSLATED FROM THE NAVAJO BY JEROME K. ROTHENBURG

This can be used as a call and response,
with the crowd calling 'may I walk'

From Invocation of Peace

Deep peace, pure white of the moon to you;
Deep peace, pure green of the grass to you;
Deep peace, pure brown of the earth to you;
Deep peace, pure grey of the dew to you;
Deep peace, pure blue of the sky to you!
Deep peace of the running wave to you,
Deep peace of the flowing air to you,
Deep peace of the quiet earth to you.

FIONA MACLEOD

Growing Pains
For Jo on her 13th birthday

A clarinet is laughing in a room
upstairs. The rain's set in, a dismal day,
though right outside there is a patch of green
that might just be a metaphor for joy –
the way it's always there despite the pain
if we can see it, waiting to be seen.

You have your mother's way of making friends.
You notice other people. It's a gift,
like being musical or good at sport.
I see you walk towards me on the lawn.
You smile and say you feel much better now.
You find the grass is greener than you thought.

PHILIP LYONS

Swimming the Quarry
For my daughter at fourteen

Taking the turquoise veil
you sleeve below the surface
on your back, wedding water. Turn,

and there's only your shadow
sunk in its element, fading
deeper and deeper in.

When little you used to say:
I came from under the water.
It's taking a long time and I'm

starting to catch my breath, to urge
you up; when you're born
on a whale of a time -

head-first, laughing. And I know
you've made your secret vows: to be
alive to the depths, to find

your own belief in everything.

MATTHEW BARTON

Adolescent

A chap be called a hobble-de-hoye
As be short of a man, but moor'n a boy

ANON

Christmas Night

I'm shaking these crumbs Lord
out under the stars this Christmas night.

We should have been glad in candlelight
but it's a dour face you see now
under my paper hat.

Tonight Lord your Son we celebrate;
but this girl you gave into our care –
I've cared and failed. Not at my table
can she break bread with grace.

I'm shaking Lord these crumbs out
Christmas night at the nerve end
of your starry agony.

Now you must father her, and midnight
be a touch of Mary upon her face.

PAUL MATTHEWS

Phantom

All look and likeness caught from earth,
All accident of kin and birth,
Has pass'd away. There was no trace
Of aught on that illumined face,
Upraised beneath the rifted stone
But of one spirit all her own –
She, she herself, and only she,
Shone through her body visibly.

SAMUEL TAYLOR COLERIDGE

First Love

I ne'er was struck before that hour
    With love so sudden and so sweet.
Her face it bloomed like a sweet flower
    And stole my heart away complete.
My face turned pale as deadly pale,
    My legs refused to walk away,
And when she looked "what could I ail?"
    My life and all seemed turned to clay.

And then my blood rushed to my face
    And took my sight away.
The trees and bushes round the place
    Seemed midnight at noonday.
I could not see a single thing,
    Words from my eyes did start;
They spoke as chords do from the string
    And blood burnt round my heart.

Are flowers the winter's choice?
  Is love's bed always snow?
She seemd to hear my silent voice
  And love's appeal to know.
I never saw so sweet a face
  As that I stood before:
My heart has left its dwelling place
  And can return no more.

JOHN CLARE

Romance

I

You're not serious when you're seventeen.
– One fine evening, tired of beers and lemonade,
The noisy cafes with their dazzling gleam!
– you walk below the lime-trees' green on the Parade.

The limes smell so good on fine June evenings!
The air's so sweet sometimes you close your eyes:
The wind, full of sounds – the town's nearby –
Blows the smell of beer, and the scent of vines...

II

– Then you make out a little tiny tatter
Of sombre azure framed by a twig of night,
Pierced by a fatal star, it melts, after
Soft tremblings, tiny and perfectly white...

June night! And seventeen! – You get tipsy.
The sap's champagne and blurs every feature...
You wander: you feel a kiss on your lips
That quivers there, like a tiny creature...

III

Your made heart goes Crusoeing the romances,
– where in the pale lamp's glare your eyes follow
A young girl going by with sweet little glances
Below the gloom of her father's stiffened collar…

And because she finds you immensely naïve
As by, in her little ankle boots, she trips
She turns away alertly with a quick shrug…
– and *cavatinas* die away on your lips…

You're in love. Taken till the month of August.
You're in love. – Your sonnets make her smile.
All your friends have gone: you're in bad taste.
– Then the adored, one evening, deigns to write!

That evening … you return to the café's gleam,
You call out for beer or lemonade…
– You're not serious when you're seventeen
And the lime-trees are green on the Parade.

ARTHUR RIMBAUD
TRANSLATED BY A.S. KLINE

Sensation

Through blue summer evenings, I'll go down the pathways,
Pricked by the wheat ears, trampling the short grass:
In a dream, I'll be sensing, beneath me, the freshness.
I'll let evening breezes bathe my forehead.

I'll speak not a thing: I'll think not a thing:
But infinite love will swell in my soul,
And, I'll go, far, far away, like a gypsy,
Through nature – joyful as if I had a girl.

ARTHUR RIMBAUD
TRANSLATED BY A.S.KLINE

Before Play
For Zoran Mishitch

One shuts one eye
Peers into oneself into every corner
Looks at oneself to see there are no spikes no thieves
No cuckoo's eggs

One shuts the other eye too
Crouches then jumps
Jumps high high high
To the top of oneself

Thence one drops by one's own weight
For days one drops deep deep deep
To the bottom of one's abyss

He who is not smashed to smithereens
He who remains whole and gets up whole
He plays

VASKO POPA
TRANSLATED BY ANNE PETHINGTON

Joy and woe are woven fine
A clothing for the soul divine,
Under every grief and pine
Runs a joy with silken twine.

It is right, it should be so
Man was made for joy and woe,
And when this we rightly know
Thro' the world we safely go.

WILLIAM BLAKE

Now That I Am Nothing

Custodian of the four ways
Guardian of the perimeters
Master of the centre
Heralds of the wind
Spokesman of the sea
Tribune of the square
Angel of the three sides
      Guard me now
      Build me now
      Watch me now
Now that there is nothing
Now that I know nothing
Now that I am nothing
Now that I am terribly afraid
Now that the structures concepts cities
Lie like windscreens in the laps of crazy drivers
And I struggle daily nightly every second
With fragment mind
Leering images
Riot imagination

Me with such a little knowledge
Such a little will
That only all I have
Is saying Yes

ALAN JACKSON

Wild One

To know it we must name it
So I name it: fear
To know it we must name it
So I name it: love

between these two
the world is swung
and a man is hung
and there's nothing to choose
yes nothing
so I name it: nothing
and I choose it
yes choose it

oh don't go away
stay
please stay
I stand sole
In this hole
my dance has made
but not alone
grant me your
companion
ship
wild one, brave one
be
be afraid
and choose
be
unknown to yourself
I will know you:
by your flags
      your storms
      your waking eyes

ALAN JACKSON

A Door

–If it wasn't for me, what would you be?
–A twisted twig on a dying tree.

–If it wasn't for me, what would you have done?
–Howled on the ground and sucked my thumb.

–If it wasn't for me, what would you have seen?
–Drugs and thugs and hideous obscene.

–If it wasn't for me, what would you have known?
–Cruel minds, hard hearts, and a terrible throne.

–And who do you say that I am?
–You are my Lord, disguised as a dragon
  You are my Lord disguised as a thief
  You are my Lord disguised as murder
  You are my Lord disguised as grief

–And what do you call your loss?
–Justice.
–And what do you call your suffering?
–Fire.
–And what do you call your emptiness?
–Door. A door. A door.

ALAN JACKSON

Motherless Child

Sometimes I feel like a motherless child,
Sometimes I feel like a motherless child,
Sometimes I feel like a motherless child,
A long ways from home,
A long ways from home.

Sometimes I feel like I'm almost gone,
Sometimes I feel like I'm almost gone,
Sometimes I feel like I'm almost gone,
A long ways from home,
A long ways from home.

Sometimes I feel like a feather in the air,
Sometimes I feel like a feather in the air,
Sometimes I feel like a feather in the air,
And I spread my wings and I fly,

I spread my wings and I fly.

ANON

A Welcome*

To this hearth which is a heart, welcome.

Welcome to our hearts. Welcome to our breath
    seeking to be song.

May those without a place tonight
    find welcome here.

May those without a tongue be brought to utterance.

Welcome to the stone that has no mouth to cry with.

Welcome to the leaf that trembles on the edge
    of speaking.

Welcome to the owl's high lonely questioning.

May our ears catch answers.

May the Word which hovers above our heads
    find hospitality.

May the song which crosses
between the living and the dead
be part of what we sing.

Welcome to the fabulous Names of things.

PAUL MATTHEWS

*Could be used in a confirmation celebration or rite of passage

Everyone Sang

Everyone suddenly burst out singing;
And I was filled with such delight
As prisoned birds must find in freedom,
Winging wildly across the white
Orchards and dark-green fields; on – on and out of sight.
Everyone's voice was suddenly lifted;
And beauty came like the setting sun:
My heart was shaken with tears; and horror
Drifted away … but everyone
Was a bird; and the song was endless; the singing will never be done.

SIEGFRIED SASSOON

Be horn

Be horn of plenty, heart,
Be skyey, never counting costs;
Be prodigal as rain, and brave.
For the law is this:
The more love let out of the horn
The more tumbles out behind.
Though we lose the way
And dark clasps us,
How warm the breath still,
How the pain shines.

GABRIEL MILLAR

I AM GOOD FORTUNE:
LEAVING HOME

Not, of course, as straightforward and final as it sounds: perhaps there will be many first flights and returns. But leaving the valley you were nurtured in, climbing the slopes and looking back from different perspectives, saying farewell and feeling the road rise beneath you – is both sweet and melancholy.

From The Kalevala

But his father straight forbade him,
Both his father and his mother,
Thence to Väinölä to journey,
That he might contend with Väinö.
'He will surely sing against you,
Sing against you, and will ban you,
Sink your mouth and head in snow-drifts,
And your hands in bitter tempest:
Till your hands and feet are stiffened,
And incapable of motion.'
Said the youthful Joukahainen,
'Good the counsel of my father,
and my mother's counsel better:
Best of all my own opinion.
I will set myself against him,
And defy him to a contest,
I myself my songs will sing him,
I myself will speak my mantras…

TRANSLATED BY W. F. KIRBY

My Bohemia: A Fantasy

I ran off, fists in my ragged seams:
Even my overcoat was becoming Ideal:
I went under the sky, Muse! I was yours:
Oh, what miraculous loves I dreamed!

My only pair of pants was a big hole.
– Tom Thumb the dreamer, sowing the roads there
with rhymes. My inn the sign of the Great Bear.
– My stars in the sky rustling to and fro.

I heard them, squatting by the wayside,
In September twilights, there I felt the dew
Drip on my forehead, like a fierce coarse wine.

Where, rhyming into the fantastic dark,
I plucked, like lyre strings, the elastics
Of my tattered shoes, a foot pressed to my heart.

ARTHUR RIMBAUD
TRANSLATED BY A.S.KLINE

A Child Leaves Home
For Mike

I grieve for your dead childhood:
abandoned, an empty casing, a chrysalis.
A few of your things remain, too trivial
or precious for your maiden flight,
and, talisman in safe hidey-holes,
I squirrel them away: while they stay,
you must return. After we left you,
your wings folded quietly by your sides,
looking forlorn, almost untried, I cried
for your fragility. That capsule of time
encases me still, a hard case from which
I will only crack free when you return;
and I admire your wing-span.

OLIVIA BYARD

From into the heart

Dreams, dreams as he rides – awake. Twilight comes into his
mind, twilight-memory, but then as he remembers, it is now: and
it is sweet.

The sun begins to go down over the heather. He shifts down into
a low gear with a flick of his boot, and brings the bike up slowly.

And then, there at the hill's top – the heather, flooded in amber, across the valley hillside, and a handful of sheep grazing, and a cottage ruin with its roof-slats lit up in the glow: then, there as he stops, and lifts the bike back onto its stand, and stands: then as he sees the light blazing over the heather … he knows - he knows nothing dies.

He knows as he knew in the garden, and he knows this time it is beauty. It is beauty it is blood and it is alive. He is alive. He is in love. With who? With what? With this. He is standing in it. He is standing in it, and it is inside him and outside him and it is the same thing. And the air is warm and still and the sun is turning rose, and he can see to the end of his journey.

And he doesn't want to go.

Night falling as gently as moth wings. Faces round a fire. It continues, as it must … and it sinks like rain, down behind his eyes, down into the ground of him. And one face reminds him. And then another. And it flows like a stream, glimmering and fading – and it grows like a well and like a hunger.

For one who has seen the rose, nothing less than it will do.

And if he is standing there now, he is reaching open his hands – and the light flows through them … the light there is no holding.

And there is only this: that his heart grows more and more like it.

Like yours, brother, gone now, into the sun. Like yours, mother.

And so he goes on down, over the hill.

JAY RAMSAY

The Traveller
After Li Po

Where do you come from? Where are you going?
It is not the world as you see it –
I have different eyes from yours

And I cross your path like a shadow.
What is it you really need?
What is that weight around your shoulders?
Who gave you that complacent smile?

I know a different kind of kingdom
Where all I carry is the sky and the moment
And people are as they are, like me,
And birds and bees and flowers are equal.

Fool, minstrel, tramp – I am all of these.
But my secret is that I am no one
And the breeze that blows through me is the breeze
And my vanishing breath on the wind.

What I give, I give. It is all I have –
And the miracle is that it's enough.

JAY RAMSAY

Definitions

North, we go north,
beyond the blue reach
of the long, consoling sky.
Away from our first home,
from the place of arrival,
the valley whose belly is fat to infinity,
laden, a fig tree,
the valley half-lidded
with futures.
Here everything
is or could be:
preposterous toucan,
or a woman suckling serpents.

But we are not for here.
We are for the north
and the scrupulous cold,
black ink
and the wind's definitions.

GABRIEL MILLAR

The Fool

The way he does it is this:
when he comes to a river
    he takes a bridge
    out of his pocket
    and walks across.

GABRIEL MILLAR

Fairy Tale

He built himself a house
    his foundations,
    his stones,
    his walls,
    his roof overhead,
    his chimney and smoke,
    his view from the window.

He made himself a garden,
    his fence,
    his thyme,
    his earthworm,
    his evening dew.

He cut out his bit of sky above.

And he wrapped the garden in the sky
and the house in the garden
and packed the lot in a handkerchief
and went off
lone as an arctic fox
through the cold
unending
rain
into the world.

Miroslav Holub
Translated by George Theiner

From Song of the Open Road

Afoot and light-hearted I take to the open road,
Healthy, free, the world before me,
The long brown path before me leading wherever I choose.
Henceforth I ask not good fortune, I myself am good fortune,
Henceforth I whimper no more, postpone no more, need nothing,
Done with indoor complaints, libraries, querulous criticisms,
Strong and content I travel the open road.
The earth, that is sufficient,
I do not want the constellations any nearer,
I know they are very well where they are,
I know they suffice for those who belong to them.

WALT WHITMAN

Daughter

It doesn't matter that she's twenty-two,
I still bargain with God
over her safe arrival
on the coach from France –
if she doesn't come back safe,
I will never again believe the angel
when he says she will never be mugged
or murdered. He said that once when she was sixteen
and out all night, with school the next day.

No it doesn't matter that my breasts
no longer leak when she cries,
and I am not on the qui vive all night
for her call. She calls and says, I'm back,
and I cook the fennel and the fatted nut roast,
light the candle, and stand for the hallelujah chorus,
fortissimo as she walks through the door.

GABRIEL MILLAR

Benedico

That earth and what is human should not stifle.
That the heart should be greater than the head:
that the spirit should be more than mind alone:
that the body should itself remain sacred.
That the earth should not die from commerce,
or the love of the earth become trade,
that the violence of the mind should be defeated,
as much as the violence of the flesh.
That every rage should be a rage of light.

That the poem should remain greater than the poet,
and the highest values be love and freedom,
and never the one without the other.
That we should go naked through all being,
and all of being nakedly through us.
That we should learn to hate our prisons and our chains,
that we should learn how to love and to be free,
and know all human futures are in freedom,
and the future of the mind to be in love.

A.S.KLINE

May the road rise to meet you,
May the wind be always at your back,
May the sun shine warm upon your face,
The rain fall soft upon your fields,
And until we meet again
May God hold you
In the palm of his hand.

ANON

APPENDIX
WALDORF SCHOOL VERSES

Rudolf Steiner (1861-1925), some of whose verses are included in the main body of this book, wrote a large number of meditations to sustain and strengthen people at different times in their lives (see *Meditations* series, Sophia Books, Rudolf Steiner Press 2002). 'Waldorf' or Rudolf Steiner schools throughout the world use many such verses, which Steiner and others wrote for children to speak at different ages and on different occasions. They affirm the relationship of each child to the surrounding world and the intangible spirit alive within it. The practice of sharing a daily verse together in the classroom gives children a sense both of cohesion with each other and of being enfolded in a greater scheme of things. It offers moments of tranquillity and can also be a way of marking transitions in the day. Waldorf Schools do not expect or wish children to subscribe to any religious dogma, but to find their own beliefs (or lack of them) as they grow older. However, Steiner – like many others – recognised that the young child is innately religious in the widest, non-sectarian sense, and his verses attempted to address what he saw as this deep need. Below are a few of them.

Morning verse for younger classes

The sun with loving light
makes each day bright for me
the soul with spirit power
fills my limbs with strength;

In sunlight shining clear
I revere O God
the human strength which you
so graciously have planted
within my soul; so that
with all my might I may
love to work and learn.
From you pour light and strength,
to you flow love and thanks.

RUDOLF STEINER

Morning verse for older classes

I look into the world –
the radiant sun,
the shimmering stars,
the solid rocks;
the life of growing plants
the living, sensing creatures:
this world, where our souls
give spirit dwelling-place;

I look into my soul
that dwells alive within.
The spirit of God weaves through
light of sun and soul:
out in the world's expanse,
within, in depths of soul.

To you O spirit of God
I turn and ask
that strength and blessing grow
within me, flow into
my learning and my work.

RUDOLF STEINER

Verse for the beginning of religious studies lessons

With those bright rays of sunlight
that make the earth abound
with that bright green of grasses
that spring from darkest ground
and where the stars inhabit
their homes in heavenly height
and in my eye where shines
the weaving force of light:
there I sense the working of God
that dawns on me in spirit
to whom in depths of soul my whole
being I unite
so that spirit comes to birth
in my being here on earth.

RUDOLF STEINER

Verse for ending a lesson

Strong are my arms
Wakeful my head
Warm be my heart
And firm be my tread.

ANON

SOME IDEAS FOR USING THIS BOOK

The only rule of thumb in reading poems, either to oneself or out loud, is to make time and space for them, allow them to work on you. You may find more there than the poet ever knew. In our busy, clamouring world, poems can be springs of reflection to gather at and draw from, havens and islands.

When speaking poems aloud to others, perhaps to young children, choose only one at a time, and leave space around it. A poem is rich fare, and swallowing too many at once may mean none are really absorbed. Poems are special occasions, heightened moments. We cannot live at that altitude all the time but we can climb to it now and then, before descending again to the run of the mill.

Savour the sounds of a poem, its music and rhythms. Each poem is a river that flows, meets obstacles, finds ways through and over, rattles its pebbles, has swift undercurrents or deep, slow places.

If you enjoy the sounds, sense and life in a poem, others you share it with will feel your enjoyment and take to it like Rilke's swan to the water (see page 154). No need to have a serious sense that children *ought* to appreciate certain poems – they simply will if you do. Or if they don't, at least they'll absorb your pleasure and remember it.

When teaching poems to young children, just speak them aloud yourself first, perhaps the same poem each day for a week or so. Young children naturally want to join in and imitate, and can learn a poem by drinking it in from you. They love hearing the same poem, song or story again and again.

Morning verses
You can speak some of these verses while a child still lies in bed – perhaps after drawing the curtains to let the day shine in - or while he or she gets out of bed and gets dressed. Nothing formal or serious:

morning verses can have a light and lovely feel, and children should feel free and easy with them. Saying a poem may seem a little awkward to you to begin with, but if you keep a gentle and playful sense in yourself and the quality in your voice, this will soon become a treasured moment for children, and one they gladly join in with.

Graces

Saying a grace is not fashionable, but it can create a lovely moment of togetherness, a brief hush of reflection which gives the rest of the meal all the more warmth and conviviality. Holding hands while speaking a grace together reinforces this communal sense. Children should not be *required* to say a grace, but will *want* to join in if they sense adults meaning something true by it. Again, there should be an easy naturalness to it, nothing starch collared or straight laced. If a family develops a repertoire of graces, children may also want to choose one each mealtime and perhaps say it on their own, when they're old enough or ready to.

Evening verses

Saying an evening verse or poem with a child has a quite different quality to speaking a morning verse. Where morning verses have a cheerful, uplifting, outgoing feel, evening verses smooth the way for a quiet, inward journey. They are probably best said when a child is in bed, after a story or song. You can make the moment even more special by lighting a candle and turning out the lights. It is good to feel very relaxed yourself, and let this calm flow into your voice. After the busyness of the day, these few, gently spoken words together can create a deep bond between parents and children.

Rites of passage

Nowadays we barely mark the important transitions in children's lives. A few of the poems (pages 165-168 and 176-182) in the 'The Ground to Stand On' section could be incorporated into a modern rite of passage to celebrate that often stormy voyage into independence. The form and time of such a celebration is no longer something passed on by tradition, as in tribal cultures, but would need creating and recreating in individual ways, as seems right to each family or group. It could be a very informal affair, just a gathering of people who care strongly about a particular young person or group of young people, with a few affirming, encouraging words spoken and perhaps a shared meal. Poetry and ritual were originally very closely connected, and poetry still retains a quality of 'heightened' speech which we resort to at times of strong emotion. This heightened quality may be something adults grow shy of – but we surely do young people a service by acknowledging it in them and ourselves. It is a quality they are deeply familiar with, one whose force and creativity can turn destructive or self-destructive if not expressed.

Last but not least

Nothing beats learning a poem by heart for owning and knowing it fully. Then it will be a possession you can always turn to. Even if you forget it, it will remain in you somewhere, its sense and music growing part of you, too close to see but still there nevertheless. It will enter the pulse at your wrist, the spring in your step.

ACKNOWLEDGEMENTS

I am particularly grateful to those poets and publishers (they know who they are) who asked only a very small fee, or in many cases none at all, for reprinting their work. This volume would not have been possible without their generosity.

For permission to reprint copyright material, the editor and publishers gratefully acknowledge the following authors and publishers:

Dorothy Baird

James Berry: 'Isn't My Name Magical', © James Berry 1994, from *A Caribbean Dozen*, Walker Books, reprinted by permission of Peters, Fraser & Dunlop on behalf of James Berry

Evan Boland: 'This Moment' from *In a Time of Violence*, Carcanet Press Ltd.1994

Olivia Byard: 'A Child Leaves Home' from *From A Benediction*, Peterloo Poets 1997, reproduced by permission of Peterloo Poets.

Catherine Byron: 'Let-Down' was first published by Loxwood Stoneleigh in *The Fat-Hen Field Hospital* by Catherine Byron in 1993

Charles Causley: 'I Am The Song' from *Collected Poems 1951-2000*, Picador 2000, by permission of David Higham Associates

Billy Collins: 'On Turning Ten' from *The Art of Drowning*, by Billy Collins ©1995, reprinted by permission of the University of Pittsburgh Press.

Laura Hope-Gill

Carrie Grabo

Gillie Griffin: 'Sleeping with Amy' was first published by Loxwood Stoneleigh in *Warm Bodies, Foreign Parts*, Gillie Griffin 1996 © Gillie Griffin

Miroslav Holub: 'Fairy Tale' from *Selected Poems*, translated Ian Milner and George Theiner, introduction by A. Alvarez (Penguin Books 1967). Copyright © Miroslav Holub 1967, translation copyright © Penguin Books, 1967, Reproduced by permission of Penguin Books Ltd.

Frances Horovitz: 'In Painswick Churchyard' from *Collected Poems*, Bloodaxe Books 1985

Alan Jackson: poems from *Heart of the Sun*, Open Township 1986, and *Salutations*, Polygon 1990

Kathleen Jamie: 'Prayer' (in 'Ultrasound') from *Jizzen*, Picador 1999, by permission of Macmillan Publishers Ltd..

Francesca Kalliomäki-Barton

Florence Kayll

A.S.Kline: 'Benedico' from *Looking Back At Earth*, internet publication at: www.tonykline.free-online.co.uk Translations of Rimbaud poems can be found at the same site.

Michael Laskey: 'Registers' from *Thinking of Happiness*, Peterloo Poets 1991, reproduced by permission of Peterloo Poets.

Philip Lyons

Norman MacCaig: 'Two-Year-Old' from Norman MacCaig: *Collected Poems*, published by Chatto and Windus 1997. Reprinted by permission of The Random House Group Ltd.

Louis MacNeice: 'Prayer Before Birth' from *Collected Poems*, Faber 1979, by permission of David Higham Associates

Walter de la Mare: 'Autumn', 'Silver', 'The Birthnight' and 'House of Dream' from *The Complete Poems of Walter de la Mare*, Faber 1969, by permission of the Literary Trustees of Walter de la Mare and the Society of Authors as their representative

Adrian Mitchell: 'Beattie Is Three', reprinted by permission of Peters, Fraser & Dunlop on behalf of Adrian Mitchell, with an educational health warning: Adrian Mitchell asks that none of his poems be used in connection with any examination whatsoever. © Adrian Mitchell 1997

John Mole: 'The Shoes' from *Catching the Spider*, Blackie 1990, by permission of the author

Jeremy Mulford

Brien Masters: 'Russet Leaves' from *Weft for the Rainbow*, the lanthorn press, 1983

Paul Matthews: poems from *The Ground That Love Seeks*, Five Seasons Press, 1996, available from Paul Matthews c/o Emerson College, Forest Row, Sussex

Gabriel Millar: from *The Saving Flame*, Five Seasons Press/Tumbled Stone Press, 2001; and *The Brook Runs*, Wynstones Press, ISBN 0 946206 09 0

Winnie Mossman

Brian Patten: 'Yes' from *Storm Damage*, Flamingo 1988, reproduced by permission of the author c/o Rogers, Coleridge and White Ltd., 20 Powis Mews, London W11 1JN

Catherine Peters

Vasko Popa: 'Before Play' is taken from *Vasko Popa: Collected Poems* translated by Anne Pennington, revised and expanded by Francis R Jones. Published by Anvil Press Poetry in 1997

Tom Pow: from *Red Letter Day*, Bloodaxe Books 1996, by permission of the author

Jay Ramsay: poems from: *For Now*, The Diamond Press 1991; *the I Ching – the shamanic oracle of change*, Thorsons 1995; *Kingdom of the Edge – Poems for the Spirit*, Element Books 1999

John Crowe Ransom: 'Janet Waking' from *Selected Poems*, Carcanet Press Ltd.

INDEX OF FIRST LINES

MATTHEW BARTON

Matthew Barton worked for many years as class teacher and then kindergarten teacher at the Bristol Waldorf School. He has taught creative writing in a prison, primary schools and at Bristol University, and worked in education welfare. Currently he is a full-time translator, editor, teacher and writer. His first collection of poems, *Learning To Row*, was published by Peterloo in 1999. His second collection is due out in 2005. He has won numerous prizes for his work, including the BBC Wildlife Poet of the Year Award, 2nd prize in the National Poetry Competition, an Arts Council Writer's Award and a Hawthornden Fellowship. He lives in Bristol with his partner, a stained glass artist, his three stepsons, daughter and grandson.